Fair Trade?

Its Prospects as a Poverty Solution

Victor V. Claar

Foreword by Michael W. Kruse

Edited by Anthony B. Bradley

PovertyCure Series

PovertyCure Series

Fair Trade?

© 2012 by PovertyCure

The PovertyCure initiative is managed by the Acton Institute.

Acton Institute
for the Study of Religion and Liberty
All rights reserved.

Cover image: "Coffee Beans & Kibera Still Life"
by Simon Scionka

ISBN 10: 1-880595-42-7
ISBN 13: 978-1-880595-42-8

British Library Cataloguing in Publication Information Available

Library of Congress Cataloging-in-Publication Data

Claar, Victor. V.

Fair Trade? Its Prospects as a Poverty Solution / Victor V. Claar

poverty cure
From aid to enterprise

161 Ottawa Avenue, NW, Suite 301
Grand Rapids, Michigan 49503
Phone: 616-454-3080
Fax: 616-454-9454
www.povertycure.org

Printed in the United States of America

Contents

Preface

The PovertyCure series is a collection of monographs and other short books focused on economic development, poverty alleviation, and entrepreneurial solutions to poverty. The plan for the series is to include a mix of new books, reissued monographs, and reprints of older works from seminal thinkers in economic development. We are grateful to the Acton Institute for permission to reprint several monographs within this series.

The purpose of the PovertyCure series is to provide further materials for research into foundational and topical issues related to poverty and development.

The authors—who include economists, moral philosophers, and practitioners—take seriously the integration of economics on the one hand with moral philosophy and theology on the other. Their work is rooted in the Judeo-Christian vision of the human person as made in the image of God with creative capacity.

About PovertyCure

PovertyCure is an international network of organizations and individuals seeking to ground our common battle against global poverty in a proper understanding of the human person and society, and to encourage solutions that foster opportunity and unleash the entrepreneurial spirit that already fills the developing world.

There is no single solution to poverty, and good people will disagree about methods, but we have joined together to rethink poverty, encourage discussion and debate, promote effective compassion, and advance entrepreneurial solutions to poverty informed by sound economics, local knowledge, the lessons of history, and reflections from the Judeo-Christian tradition.

Christ calls us to solidarity with the poor, but this means more than assistance. It means seeing the poor not as objects or experiments, but as partners and brothers and sisters, as fellow human beings made in the image of God with the capacity to solve problems and create new wealth for themselves and their families. At a practical level, it means inviting, and being invited into, broader circles of exchange and productivity.

The PovertyCure initiative seeks to spread this integrated message through a seven-session curriculum, a multimedia website, a documentary, and our international network of partner organizations working in everything from microfinance to clean water, orphanages, and business investment.

We hope you find the books in the series valuable and encourage you to visit Povertycure.org to learn more, or go to Povertycure.org/network to learn how individuals and organizations can join PovertyCure in the work of transforming charity and development.

Michael Matheson Miller
PovertyCure

Foreword

A common theme runs through Scripture and on through the history of the Church: concern for the poor. Individually and corporately, we are called to seek the welfare of the poor. Consensus on how to answer this call has varied as cultures and contexts change. As we begin the twenty-first century, a noticeable shift has occurred in the response American Christians are giving to this call.

For post-World War II America, compassionate service was achieved through large centralized organizations. Businesses and workers gave unrestricted donations to the local United Way that strategically allocated resources to nonprofit enterprises. Church members dutifully sent their contributions to a national church office to coordinate ministry on behalf of congregants. It was best to let the professionals handle it. Much has changed.

For a great many people today, impersonally funding services is insufficient. There must be a personal experiential connection. Compassion International developed a model linking donors with specific children. Habitat for Humanity created a model where volunteers get their hands dirty building homes for the poor. More recently, *Kiva.com* created a microfinance service where people make small enterprise loans to specific individuals in emerging nations, and, of course, there is the explosion of short-term mission trips by a wide range of American congregations.

Parallel to these changes has been a growing interest in discerning how our personal actions affect the economy, society, and the environment. Consumerism is seen as a threat to material and spiritual qualities of life. While Christians have a history of organizing against perceived corporate and governmental injustice, individuals are now cognizant of how their personal economic decisions impact the world. What we buy and how we buy it is integral to our spiritual development and Christian witness.

Fair trade is a prominent expression of this desire to influence the world through personal economic decisions. Poor farmers and small-crafts producers in emerging nations who agree to certain social and environmental standards can have their products certified as "fair trade" goods by various organizations. Compassionate and just consumers in developed nations willingly pay a premium for these fair trade goods, intending to create a better life for the producers.

These fair trade strategies have been emerging since World War II, but interest has really blossomed over the last twenty years. Religious organizations and confessional groups, particularly communions connected with the National Council of Churches, have been avid supporters of fair trade goods. For instance, within my own church, the Presbyterian Church, U.S.A., there is the Presbyterian Coffee Project, which also sells cocoa and chocolate. It operates in cooperation with Equal Exchange, a fair trade distributor. Congregations are encouraged to promote fair trade coffee to their congregants and to their communities. The Presbyterian Coffee Exchange website (http://www.pcusa.org/coffee/) says:

Participating congregations testify that the Presbyterian Coffee Project is a great way to help people in need while enjoying fellowship and an excellent cup of coffee. Fair trade practices complement our mission with farmers in Latin America, Africa and Asia, as well as our commitment to stewardship of the natural environment. By using fair trade coffee in our congregations, offices and homes, Presbyterians help guarantee that farmers will earn the income they need to feed their families, educate their children and improve their communities. Fair trade is a simple solution that means the difference—quite literally—between surviving and not surviving for small-scale coffee farmers.

The appeal of these programs is the sense of personal connection that participants develop when fighting injustice. There is little doubt that most who participate are acting out of an honest desire to reshape the world in a way that honors God and aids the poor. The question that is rarely critically examined, however, is whether or not fair trade programs actually deliver on their economic promises.

Part of the problem is the moralistic way the issue is framed. After all, who supports "unfair trade?" We might well ask how fair trade differs from free trade. What is the unfairness that fair trade rectifies? Many fair trade advocates name farm subsidies in wealthy nations as an example of unfairness. Farm subsidies keep domestic goods artificially cheap, thus making imported goods from poor nations uncompetitive. Others protest that many goods are harvested or manufactured with forced labor. Yet, by definition, free trade is exchange between parties that are free of government interference (like tariffs and subsidies) and where parties are free of coercion. Calling for the elimination of subsidies and an end to forced labor is advocacy for *free trade*.

Frequently, there is simply a general sentiment among fair traders that market exchange inherently *causes*, or at least contributes to, the poverty of peasants. A fairer exchange system is desired. The economic analysis goes little deeper than this. Yet, as disciples of Jesus Christ, called to exercise compassion and seek justice, sentiment and good intentions are not enough. We must scrutinize our actions to see if they achieve the ends we intend. If they do not achieve our ends, we risk the perverse circumstance of damaging the people we intend to help, even as we seek personal solidarity with their suffering.

With fair trade, we are looking at an economic question. What might an economic analysis of fair trade tell us? Victor Claar offers us vital insights.

Michael W. Kruse
Author of the Kruse Kronicle blog
http://krusekronicle.typepad.com/
Chair
General Assembly Mission Council
Presbyterian Church (U.S.A.)

1 Introduction*

Buying fair trade goods is perhaps the most visible recent initiative intended to improve the lot of the global poor, and also one that has been particularly embraced by the Christian community throughout much of the wealthy first world. While the strength of the embrace varies across Christendom, fair trade has been welcomed especially strongly in mainline protestant denominations, the Catholic Church, and the emerging church movement. Although it is rare to find much common ground among these three groups, they appear quite united in their belief that their purchase of fair trade goods will make a significant difference in the lives of the global poor. Additionally, while the fair trade movement includes a broad variety of goods and services, fair trade has enjoyed its greatest growth and recent success in the production, sales, and marketing of coffee.

The idea behind buying fair trade is a simple, compassionate one. Rich northern consumers pay a little extra for coffee that has been certified to satisfy fair trade standards by one of the member groups of the Fairtrade Labelling Organizations International (FLO). Through their purchases of fair trade coffee, consumers presumably engage in "ethical consumption," using the coffee market itself as a means of voting for better treatment of southern coffee growers. The primary guarantee of the fair trade label is that the coffee bearing its mark has been produced by individual or family growers—working within a cooperative—who receive a minimum-price guarantee for their crop. For example, fair trade coffee growers of washed arabica (high quality) coffee are currently guaranteed a minimum price of US$1.25 per pound, plus an additional ten cents per pound paid as a "social premium" intended for local community and business development projects such as schools, sanitation, or health care. When the world price of coffee rises above $1.25, the growers receive the world price plus the social premium. Lower-quality robusta beans are fair-trade eligible as well, but the guaranteed price is lower.

Mainline protestants have been especially active in buying and promoting fair trade coffee through their participation in the Interfaith Program offered by Equal Exchange, a Massachusetts-based for-profit fair trade coffee roaster and distributor. Through its Interfaith Program, Equal Exchange sells and distributes its products through a network of concerned Protestant congregations. Participating churches may purchase coffee from Equal Exchange at the same wholesale prices paid by retailers, and then sell the products to church members. Churches are also encouraged to serve Equal Exchange's coffees during their fellowship hours. In the case with which the author is personally most familiar, members of the congregation's Global Outreach Committee take charge of advertising fair trade coffee in the weekly bulletins and monthly newsletters, placing orders for their inventory with Equal Exchange, and staffing a cart each Sunday where parishioners can conveniently purchase fair trade coffees and other Equal Exchange products. The committee has even put together special seasonal bundles designed for gift-giving.

The Equal Exchange Interfaith Program is broad and growing. A partial list of its current protestant partners is given here:

Church of the Brethren Coffee Project
Disciples of Christ Coffee Project
Lutheran World Relief Coffee Project
Mennonite Central Committee Coffee Project
Presbyterian Coffee Project
United Church of Christ Coffee Project
United Methodist Committee on Relief Coffee
    Project
Unitarian Universalist Service Committee Coffee
    Project

In July 2005, the *Presbyterian Record*, the monthly magazine of the Presbyterian Church of Canada, devoted its entire issue to fair trade. The issue included a fair trade editorial; a feature entitled, "Mad about the Bean: Fair Trade Is Good to the Last Drop"; and a short article by Canadian broadcaster, author, and speaker Michael Coren. On the editor's page, David Harris claims that "[t]here's no excuse not to serve fair trade."[1] Coren's piece bears the title, "Christians Must Fight for Fair Trade: Loving Jesus Demands a Struggle for a Fair World Economy."[2]

The movement to buy fair trade coffee has also taken hold in Catholic circles. Philip Booth of the United Kingdom's (UK's) Institute of Economic Affairs notes that the British diocese of Arundel and Brighton declared itself to be a "Fairtrade Diocese" in June 2005.[3] The diocesan Website boasts that forty-seven of its parishes are "Fairtrade" in their own right, and notes that, "[f]or the Christian, Fairtrade can also be a help to spiritual growth." Fair trade is growing in strength among Catholics in the United States as well. For example, Catholic Relief Services operates its own Interfaith Fair Trade partnership with Equal Exchange.

The fair trade coffee initiative is especially strong among the emerging church movement in the United States.[4] Given

3

the emerging church's emphasis on reimagining how Jesus would live, serve, and minister to others in our contemporary, media-driven culture, buying fair trade coffee provides emerging groups with one more way to actively care for the global poor. This point has been made especially strongly by key emerging voices such as Brian McLaren's, founding pastor of Cedar Ridge Community Church in the Baltimore-Washington area. In his 2007 book, *Everything Must Change*, McLaren goes even further than the FLO's current coffee certification program. He writes: "My personal proposal: that we create an international fair trade seal (like the Good Housekeeping Seal of Approval) that could rate any product or service based on the ethics of its production. This seal would help people who want to engage in ethical buying and compare products."[5] Similarly Shane Claiborne, another author with significant sway among emergents, champions fair trade in his 2006 bestseller from Zondervan, *The Irresistible Revolution: Living as an Ordinary Radical*.

Thus, the fair trade coffee movement is strong among Christians of many varieties in these first years of the new millennium. For many, the decision to buy fair trade coffee is not really a decision at all—it is a commitment. Buying coffee for a premium price is viewed by most fair trade advocates as an act of justice carried out though the operations of free trade in international markets. The fair trade act is an act of "dollar democracy" in which coffee demanders see themselves as standing up in the face of injustices that have been visited on poor small-scale coffee growers by either greedy multinational corporations (MNCs) or greedy middlemen who pay growers less than the "just" price for the coffee they honestly grow and harvest.

This short book explores the modern fair trade coffee network from the perspective of a Christian concerned for the plight of the world's poorest people and follows the following plan. The next chapter lays out the essential facts about the coffee industry and the determination of coffee prices in the absence of fair trade. This is followed by a brief history of the fair trade movement, explaining how we have arrived at its current incarnation. After laying that careful groundwork, the analysis turns to an examination of the claims of the fair trade network and whether it can be expected to deliver on its promises. The book closes by considering how an informed Christian may thoughtfully, carefully, and lovingly respond to the fair trade coffee network and its champions.

The plight of the global poor is not good. It should daily break our hearts that in our modern world of abundant food, technology, and other resources we have not done a better job of enabling the poorest among us to enjoy even the most basic goods and services most of us take for granted—things such as clean water, food for today, sanitation, and basic education and medicine. I am convinced that real, long-term hope for today's global poor lies in our united prayerful anticipation of the day in which we will no longer think in terms of "us" (wealthy Westerners) and "them" (the global poor). Instead, the question that should gnaw at us most deeply is how we can each be effective forces to bring about a world in which such a distinction is no longer relevant—a world in which all people share together, with enduring personal dignity and freedom, the blessings and rich abundance of God's gracious and innumerable gifts intended for us all.

This monograph, then, brings economic thinking to bear on ethical considerations of immense importance. Nevertheless, the approach is one of both humility and reverence: humility regarding what economics can and cannot illuminate, and reverence for God and all of his creatures. As Tim Harford has marvelously put it, "[a]n economist cannot solve ... ethical conundrums, but economics can unwrap them so that at least the ethical questions become clearer."[6]

Notes

* The author thanks Robin J. Klay for helpful comments on an earlier draft.
1 David Harris, "Raise a Mug for Fair Trade," *Presbyterian Record* (May 4, 2004).
2 Michael Coren, "Christians Must Fight for Fair Trade," *Presbyterian Record* (May 2005).
3 Philip Booth, "Fairly Dangerous: The Church Takes a Stand against Free Traders," Acton Commentary (December 1, 2004), http://www.acton.org/commentary/commentary_231.php.
4 For those unfamiliar with the emerging-church phenomenon, an excellent survey of the movement in both the United States and the United Kingdom is given by Eddie Gibbs and Ryan K. Bolger, *Emerging Churches: Creating Christian Community in Postmodern Cultures* (Grand Rapids: Baker Academic, 2005).
5 Brian D. McLaren, *Everything Must Change: Jesus, Global Crises, and a Revolution of Hope* (Nashville, Tenn.: Thomas Nelson, 2007), 325.
6 Tim Harford, *The Undercover Economist* (Oxford, UK: Oxford University Press, 2006), 53.

II What Is the Problem? Essentials of the Coffee Market

Before exploring the specifics of the fair trade network today, it is important to develop an essential understanding of the coffee market. After all, if fair trade advocates argue that coffee is a market that deserves a unique approach, then a better understanding of what makes it unique will be helpful as we consider the potential of fair trade to improve standard free-market outcomes.

Bean Basics: Arabicas and Robustas

Broadly speaking, there are two varieties of coffee: arabica and robusta. Milder *arabicas* (*Coffea arabica*) are grown at high elevations and are prized for their mellow flavor. Because arabicas thrive at higher elevations, they tend to do especially well among the nations of Latin America, including Colombia, Brazil, and Guatemala. Arabicas are also naturally suited to small-scale production because the surrounding terrain may make plantation-scale plantings and harvesting difficult.

Robusta (*Coffea canephora*) beans are more bitter, their plants are hardier (more robust), and they can be grown in a much broader variety of locales. Robustas are also more resistant to insects and fungi that can damage a coffee crop, while packing a greater caffeine punch. Robustas gained their first serious market growth spurt after GIs returned home from World War II and were seeking the instant coffee they had drunk during wartime—a coffee produced mainly with robustas. Robustas are frequently included among blended coffees sold to consumers and are growing in their global production. Important robusta producers include many nations in Africa and southern Asia, such as Angola, Uganda, and Vietnam—a country that has recently exploded onto the world stage as a major robusta grower.

From Grower Through the Roasting Process

Once growers pick the green coffee "cherries" that they harvest—often by hand—the beans must be prepared for shipment. The processing must begin within twenty-four hours of harvesting; otherwise, the cherries begin to ferment.[1] There are two processing methods available: dry and wet.

In the *dry* method, developed in Brazil, green cherries are stripped from their branches and then spread on patios to dry, where they are turned several times each day. Once dry, the beans are pounded to remove the dry and shriveled husks and parchment, dramatically reducing the shipping weight of the unroasted bean. Today about 40 percent of arabicas are processed using the dry method, coming from countries such as Ethiopia and Paraguay, as well as Brazil. This method is thought to produce poor-quality beans because both ripe and unripe cherries are prepared together and because beans can grow moldy while drying.

Originally developed in Central America and Colombia, the *wet* method, while labor-intensive, produces a higher-quality average bean. The husks are removed by machine, and then the beans are soaked in water for as much as two days in order to remove the parchment from each. Beans are then dried, either in heated rotating machines or in the sun. Next, the beans are hand-sorted to remove any moldy, broken, or otherwise poor-quality beans. Today most non-Brazilian mild arabicas are processed using the wet method.

These are the final stages of production for coffee intended for export. While coffee roasting—the required next step—could presumably provide considerable income to coffee-exporting nations, roasting is done only after the coffee has arrived in the markets in which it will be sold because beans grow stale faster once they have been roasted.[2]

The Fundamentals of the Coffee Market

There are many goods that frequently experience wide fluctuations in their prices. Perhaps the one we notice most because it affects us so regularly is the price of gasoline.

What is it about some commodities—like gasoline—that makes their prices move so far over such short time horizons? The answer lies in an economic concept known as *price elasticity*. Price elasticities describe how quickly the actions of either buyers or sellers change in response to some initial price movement.

Think about how your own decision regarding how much gasoline to buy next week would change if next week, when you visit your local station, you discover that the price of gasoline is 20 percent higher than it was this week. Now, economists everywhere deeply believe that higher prices will lead consumers to purchase less of a good. We are so convinced of the reliability of this inverse relationship between the price of a good and the quantity consumers are interested in buying that we call it the *law* of demand.

If you do find yourself next week at your local gasoline station with an empty tank, will you purchase less than you had been planning to when you see that prices are 20 percent higher? You probably will buy less, but probably not much less. After all, you will be driving the same car next week you are driving this week, and it will get the same mileage that it got this week. You will still face the same distances from your home to your work, your children's schools, your church, and the grocery. Therefore, perhaps you will buy less gasoline but maybe *just a little less;* faced with a 20 percent rise in prices you might reduce your weekly gallons purchased by, say, 2 percent.

When consumers behave this way—changing the quantity they purchase by a small percentage in response to a relatively hefty percentage change in the price, we say that their demand is *inelastic*—almost unresponsive. Other goods with demand that tends to be price inelastic include addictive substances such as alcohol and tobacco, insulin for diabetics, milk for young families, or the electricity that heats your home. Even when price swings are large—whether up or down—consumers simply do not change, by much, anyway, their buying patterns for goods such as these.

Where coffee drinkers are concerned, coffee has a lot in common with goods like milk, insulin, tobacco, and alcohol. If coffee prices rise, coffee drinkers will probably buy less coffee but probably not much less. One source suggests that when the price of coffee rises by 1 percent, the quantity of coffee demanded by coffee-drinkers falls be a mere 0.3 percent.[3] When coffee prices fall, consumers generally do not change their cups-per-day in response either.[4]

This means that the number of cups of coffee consumed by coffee drinkers is price-inelastic—not very responsive to changes in the price of coffee. What about the supply of coffee? How quickly can the supply of coffee rise if prices happen to increase? That is, how responsive can coffee suppliers be in responding to price movements?

Return to the gas station. In any given week, our nation has a fixed number of oil refineries in service, as well as a fixed number of available wells in operation. If oil companies discover that the price of gasoline has risen by 20 percent, they will respond with more gasoline, but they are limited in their ability to supply *much* more in the short-term. Perhaps, therefore, from one week to the next a 20 percent rise in the price of gasoline leads to a 4 percent increase in the quantity of available gasoline. If so, then we say that the *supply* is *price-inelastic*.

It turns out that the supply of coffee is price-inelastic too. Because of the nature of the coffee market, it is difficult for coffee growers to respond quickly and supply more coffee at higher prices—even though that is exactly what they would love to do (supply more as prices rise). For example, suppose that coffee prices are on the rise, and growers in the southern hemisphere would like to respond by growing more coffee. There will likely be an increase in the quantity of coffee supplied, but it will not be by much—at least in the short-term. New robusta plants require two to three years to reach maturity for harvest, while new Arabica plants mature in three to five years.[5] The news is not much better if the price moves in the opposite direction. Once mature, a new coffee plant will yield coffee for about a decade.[6]

Coffee production has its own parallel to the refining capacity of the gasoline market. At any given time, there is a limited roasting capacity for coffee. Today most coffee roasting is done by three major players: Kraft General Foods, part of Philip Morris and owner of Maxwell House; Proctor & Gamble, roasters of Folgers and Millstone; and Sara Lee, producer of the Chock full o'Nuts and Hills Bros. brands.[7] Just like an oil refinery has a capacity that is fixed at any moment in time, coffee roasters also have a limited refining capacity over the near term. Thus, even if prices were rising dramatically, coffee roasters would not be able to supply all the coffee they would like. They will supply more, just not much more.

Therefore, the supply of coffee is price-inelastic: Growers cannot quickly change the amount of coffee they grow in a short time period. Additionally, the demand for coffee is also price inelastic: Coffee drinkers do not vary the quantity of coffee they drink by much as prices change.

We are now prepared to arrive at the reason why goods such as gasoline and coffee exhibit such wide variations in price over very short time frames. When the demand for a good is price-inelastic—as it is for coffee—and the supply is also highly price-inelastic, then neither side of the market can react quickly to any changes going on with the other side of the market. For example, suppose that a new study convincingly shows that more coffee drinking leads to greater longevity and happiness and that this information fundamentally changes consumers' desire for coffee. Existing coffee drinkers will want more and even a few noncoffee drinkers might decide to take up coffee-drinking. Even though there is a huge surge in demand, *in the near term the supply of coffee available remains relatively fixed*. Thus, more consumers are chasing the same—relatively fixed—quantities of coffee, leading to an eventual price spike. In this way, a change in demand can lead to a very wide swing in the price of coffee.

Now let us consider a sudden change in the supply of coffee. If an unseasonal frost kills off much of the current coffee crop, then less coffee will be available in the market. Yet *coffee-drinkers drink roughly the same number of cups each day*. What will happen? The price of the now-scarce coffee will rise rapidly, given that the same numbers of consumers are now chasing less coffee.

Thus far, we have seen that it is easy for a market to experience wide price fluctuations when both producers and consumers are slow to respond to changes happening on the other side of the market. However, the biggest price swings of all happen when the supply of coffee and the demand for coffee change in opposite directions at the same time. For example, let us put the two preceding illustrations together. Suppose that demand rises due to the promised longevity and happiness benefits, while the cold weather is simultaneously wiping out the coffee crop. In such instances, we will see the biggest price swings of all: in this case a massive price spike. Due to the interactions of inelastic demand and supply, it is not unusual for the commodity price of coffee to change by 50 to 150 percent in a very short time.[8]

By ignoring dramatic short-term spikes and drops in coffee prices, the overall trend of coffee prices has been largely downward. This has happened due to the opposite combination of that described immediately above, and over a longer period of time. Instead of drops in supply combined with increases in coffee demand, we have seen a longer-term decline in coffee demand coupled with vast increases in the global coffee supply. Despite the recent rise of the gourmet coffee industry, coffee demand overall has fallen throughout much of the second half of the twentieth century. In 1962, Americans over the age of ten drank about 3.1 cups per day. But owing largely to the expanding market share of soft drinks in the beverage market, by the 1990s a typical American drank just 1.6–1.9 cups of coffee daily.[9]

At the same time that the overall demand for coffee has been dropping, the supply of coffee has been rising—and massively so. This growth is due to several factors. The first is the increasing share of the robusta bean in the coffee market. During the 1950s, Africa began growing more robusta beans, constituting 80 percent of Africa's coffee exports. Today about 25 percent of all beans are robustas, coming mostly from Africa and Asia, as well as Brazil and Ecuador.[10]

Meanwhile, growth of robustas has exploded in Vietnam, which has vaulted onto the scene in recent years as the planet's main producer of robusta beans. Just as furniture manufacturing in Grand Rapids, Michigan, and the textile industry in New England moved to the American South in search of lower-wage workers, so coffee production is now moving to parts of the globe where wage costs are low. Coffee is also a natural business for the poor to enter because it requires little in the way of specific knowledge or expertise. During the 1990s alone, Vietnam expanded its coffee production—consisting of mostly robustas—by about 1400 percent, putting it behind Brazil as the world's second largest coffee grower.[11] More specifically, in 1990, Vietnam's production totaled 1.4 million 60Kg bags. Ten years later, output had risen to 14.8 million bags, though production has tapered more recently. By

2001, Vietnam was producing 12.3 million bags, and in 2002 it produced 8.7 million, leaving it as the world's number three coffee grower, behind only Brazil and Colombia.[12]

Low wages in the parts of the globe suitable for robusta production are not alone responsible for the world's current massive supply of coffee beans—though they are the primary source. Other factors include technological advances that lead to greater crop yields, better fertilizers used in better ways, and—as discussed above—the fact that coffee plants are perennials that yield coffee for a decade once mature. As Gavin Fridell puts it, improved technology and fertilizers have only compounded the oversupply problem.[13]

Although fertilizers and technology make the supply of coffee even greater than it would be otherwise, the primary reason that coffee prices remain low is that there is simply too much coffee being grown by vast segments of the world's global poor who will work for low wages and who have no better option currently available to them. In his book *The Undercover Economist*, *Financial Times* columnist Tim Harford puts it this way and also foreshadows the conclusion of my argument in this monograph:

> Coffee growers are poor because.... [t]here are many places where coffee can be grown. Growing mass-market coffee requires hard work but little skill.... Vietnam is a great example. A few years ago, coffee was hardly grown in the country at all, but now it is the world's second-largest producer of coffee.... [N]arrowly focused initiatives ... will never make a substantial improvement to the lives of millions.... [T]hey cannot fix the basic problem: too much coffee is being produced. At the slightest hint that coffee farming will become an attractive profession, it will always be swamped with desperate people who have no alternative.[14]

The preceding discussion has set the stage for what follows. So far, we have seen that coffee prices are subject to dramatic seasonal price spikes and drops due to the unfortunate synergy that results when demand and supply are both inelastic. We have also observed that while decreasing demand for coffee has contributed somewhat to ongoing low coffee prices, the main culprit keeping average coffee prices low is the vast amount of coffee being produced each season. The growers of coffee receive little because, while the job requires hard work, coffee can be grown in many places by desperately poor people with few skills and even fewer options, as the meteoric growth of coffee in Vietnam illustrates.

Indeed, if someone is currently growing coffee, we can safely presume that is his best available option. If it were not, he would be doing something else instead. Yet, growing coffee pays poorly. Moreover, due to the synergy of demand and supply inelasticities, a coffee grower faces tremendous risk and uncertainty at the start of a growing season because coffee prices can fluctuate dramatically over quite short periods of time. A grower simply cannot forecast with much certainty the price at which he will be able to sell his crop.

For these two reasons—low prices and high-price variability —the fair trade movement has sought to help poor coffee growers by guaranteeing both higher prices and greater price stability. In the next chapter, we unlock the origins, history, and methods of fair trade.

Notes

1. Mark Pendergrast, *Uncommon Grounds: The History of Coffee and How It Transformed Our World* (New York: Basic Books, 1999), 396.
2. Gavin Fridell, *Fair Trade Coffee: The Prospects and Pitfalls of Market-Driven Social Justice* (Toronto: University of Toronto Press, 2007), 149.
3. Robert H. Bates, *Open-Economy Politics: The Political Economy of the World Coffee Trade* (Princeton, N.J.: Princeton University Press, 1997), 176–77.
4. Although they might buy a bit extra to put in the pantry.
5. Fridell, *Fair Trade Coffee*, 117.
6. Miriam Wasserman, "Trouble in Coffee Lands," *Regional Review* (Federal Reserve Bank of Boston) 12, no. 2 (2002): 8.
7. Wasserman, "Trouble in Coffee Lands," 9.
8. Ibid., 8.
9. Ibid., 8.
10. Fridell, *Fair Trade Coffee*, 123.
11. Wasserman, "Trouble in Coffee Lands," 6.
12. Brink Lindsey, "Grounds for Complaint? Understanding the 'Coffee Crisis,'" Trade Briefing Paper No. 16 (Washington D.C.: Cato Institute, 2003), 4.
13. Fridell, *Fair Trade Coffee*, 141, 145.
14. Tim Harford, *The Undercover Economist* (Oxford, U.K.: Oxford University Press, 2006), 228–29.

III   Fair Trade Coffee

There have always been efforts by interested parties to keep coffee prices higher than they would otherwise be. The literature of economics is full of models of such maneuvers, which consist mostly of ways in which sellers attain at least some degree of "power through scarcity" over the market. As it stands today, coffee growers receive low prices for their crop because there are so many of them, each growing large amounts of coffee. Coffee prices are low because coffee growers have no power through scarcity.

One way to try to manipulate prices higher is to increase one's power through scarcity—what economists call "monopoly power." Other things being equal, scarcer goods will command higher prices. Similarly, the smaller the number of sellers of a good, the higher the price each can afford to charge. Monopolies are the simplest examples. Cartels work similarly; when they work to the long-term benefit of their members, cartels conspire to charge a price that is just as high as the price that would be charged by a lone monopolist in the same market.

17

Throughout the twentieth century, the nation of Brazil attempted to give itself power through scarcity over the price of its coffee beans. The Brazilian government routinely bought up surplus coffee beans—in much the same way that the U.S. government currently purchases surplus crops from farmers already enjoying taxpayer-funded price guarantees.

Governmental attempts to purchase power through scarcity by buying up each season's surplus leads to an inevitable problem: disposing of the surplus goods that have been purchased by using tax revenues as the means of payment. In the United States, our current solution in many cases is to go ahead and pay the farmers that we subsidize, while demanding that they simply stop growing their crops. The news media sometimes refer to this practice as "paying farmers not to grow crops," and that is an accurate description. Paying farmers not to grow crops keeps farmers secure, while also avoiding the awful disposal problem that comes along with buying up a surplus in an effort to keep prices artificially high.

The Brazilian government has pursued several methods of adding to the nation's power through scarcity over the price of coffee. In one extreme example from 1937, they burned over 17 million bags of Brazilian coffee; only 30 percent of their harvest reached the market, thus keeping prices relatively high.[1]

However, Brazil's attempts to keep prices high were ultimately undone. Just like Vietnam recently transformed itself from a nation that grew no coffee to a major player in the world market, it was ultimately Brazil's efforts to keep coffee prices high that led to the birth of Colombia as a major coffee producer. In 1900, Colombia produced just 600,000 bags of coffee. By 1932, Colombia's production had risen to 3.5 million bags.[2] Brazil was powerless to stop this process. Moreover, in looking for culprits to blame, Brazil could blame only itself. Keeping coffee prices high by burning up coffee made other nations eager to enter the coffee industry. Indeed, Vietnam is merely the Colombia of the new millennium.

While Brazil had sought power through scarcity as its path to profits, Colombia famously used marketing to emphasize the quality of their beans. Juan Valdez, the marketing hallmark of Colombia's Federación Nacional de Cafeteros (FNC), was a "friendly, mustachioed coffee grower who, with his mule, trundled his hand-picked arabica beans down from the Colombian mountains."[3] The Valdez character was introduced by the FNC in 1960 and proved to be tremendously successful in the United States, and it also left a measurable legacy. Since the 1960s, the price of Colombian coffee has generally remained higher than the prices of other arabicas.[4]

Ratified in 1963, the International Coffee Agreement (ICA) maintained considerable coffee-price stability from the mid 1960s through 1989. Brokered during difficult sessions at the United Nations's (U.N.'s) 1962 Coffee Conference, the ICA established a production quota for each of its participating nations, and the original agreement was designed to last for five years—leaving open its possible renewal. In the initial quota system, Brazil was limited to 18 million bags of coffee, Colombia's limit was 6 million bags, the Ivory Coast's initial limit was 2.3 million bags, and Angola was limited to slightly more than 2 million bags, with the remainder of the worldwide limit distributed to the other coffee-producing nations based on their past levels of production. The industry-standard bag size is 132 pounds.[5]

Gaining the support of both the U.S. government and the National Coffee Association (NCA) for the initial agreement was not difficult. In the early 1960s, the Cold War was at its most frigid. The U.S. government was concerned that Latin America—as well as Angola and other parts of Africa—was dangerously teetering toward a slide down into the Communist ravine due to the combined influences of poverty, social unrest, and the apparent willingness of Latin and other leaders to listen to Marxist ideas and pursue them—in some cases to the point of violent revolution. Hoping to keep such pressures from growing, the United States reluctantly signed onto the agreement.

As with many price-stabilization schemes, the ICA was far from perfect. Such imperfections included the problem of "tourist beans." Should a producer in a nation participating in ICA's quota system find itself with excess beans, the producer could sell its excess supply to nations such as Japan who were not participants in the ICA. Japan could then resell the beans to their eventual consumption destination, including to North American buyers.[6]

With the Soviet experiment coming to a close in the late 1980s, the ICA also fell apart. The communist threat had faded, and worldwide coffee production had grown so vast that the NCA was no longer fearful of wide price swings in the coffee market. The stage was set for the birth of the modern fair trade movement.

The Modern Fair Trade Movement

Even as the Cold War began to thaw, the U.S. government nevertheless remained concerned about isolated Marxist threats in Latin America, including Nicaragua. By 1986, the Reagan administration had imposed a complete trade embargo against Nicaragua. In solidarity with Nicaraguan coffee growers, a small for-profit cooperative in New England called Equal Exchange exploited a small loophole in the trade restrictions and began importing and roasting Nicaraguan coffee.[7]

Equal Exchange had begun just a few years earlier, created by social activists interested in bringing fairly traded coffee into the United States, initially financed by Christian groups. Since its humble beginnings, Equal Exchange has emerged as the number-one seller of fair trade coffee in the United States. By the mid-1990s, its annual sales were over $3 million.[8]

While Equal Exchange was beginning its profit-seeking fair trade importing and roasting business in the United States, the first fair trade labeling organization was being formed across the Atlantic in the Netherlands. In the late 1980s, the Unión de Comumidades Indigens de la Región del Istmo (UCIRI), a cooperative of coffee growers from the Mexican state of Oaxaca, was seeking new markets for their coffee. Large multinational companies had shown little interest in their Oaxacan beans, so UCIRI began to explore other possibilities. Working together with Solidaridad, an ecumenical foundation that extended grants to cooperatives like UCIRI, they brainstormed ways to bring their product to previously unexplored markets. Following extensive discussions between UCIRI and Solidaridad in the Netherlands during 1988, the Max Havelaar fair trade label was born. They took their name from a Dutch novel in which the hero, Max Havelaar, denounces the treatment of Indonesian coffee growers under Dutch colonial rule.[9]

Today Max Havelaar is just one of several fair trade labeling organizations spread across Western nations and is responsible for giving an assurance to Dutch coffee drinkers that their coffee cups are filled with justice. If you see the Max Havelaar mark, you know the coffee is certified as fair trade coffee. The Fair Trade Foundation performs a similar function in the United Kingdom and Ireland, and Fair Trade USA is the official fair trade referee in the United States. These three certifiers of fair trade coffees, as well as the respective national fair trade certifiers in each other importing nation, are overseen by FLO. The FLO sets forth the following guiding principles:

- Democratic organization,
- Abhorrence of exploitative child labor,
- Environmental sustainability, and
- International Labour Organization (ILO) standards for paid employees.

Responsibilities of the FLO include certifying and auditing its licensees, facilitating business contacts, and providing organizational and technical support to growers and workers.[10] FLO limits entry into the fair trade network to *cooperatives* of *small* coffee growers. This restriction means that farmers operating on larger scales are locked out of the fair trade network, regardless of the sustainability of their production methods or the humaneness of their human resource management. This dual restriction—small and part of a cooperative—implies that fair trade misses the majority of coffee growers—whether large or small.

Poor growers face two additional restrictions in gaining access to the fair trade network. First, FLO restricts the overall number of entrants into the fair trade network. That is, there is a *de facto* quota on fair trade coffee. Second, a cooperative of poor coffee farmers that aspires to enter the network must pay a hefty entry fee. In 2004, it cost each organization $3,200 to gain FLO certification.

As mentioned in the introduction, the primary goal of fair trade is to give coffee growers in the network a guaranteed minimum price. Although the fair trade pricing formula has evolved over time, fair trade coffee growers of arabica coffee are currently guaranteed $1.25 per pound, plus an additional ten cents per pound paid as a social premium intended for local community and business development projects such as schools, sanitation, and health care. Should the world price rise above $1.25, the growers receive the world price plus the social premium. Robustas are fair trade eligible as well but receive a lower price. Figure 1 depicts the world price of arabicas over the period 1980–2008, as well as the fair trade price in force during each year.

Figure 1

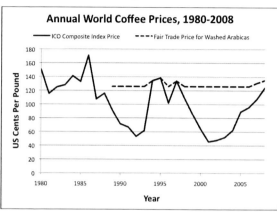

Source: The International Coffee Organization, http://www.ico.org/ new_historical.asp, and the author's own historical calculation of fair trade prices using the FLO formula.

Given our earlier discussion of elasticities of supply and demand, it is interesting to note the two large price spikes in the data. The spike in 1994 corresponds to severe frost damage in Brazil while the 1997 spike reflects a Brazilian drought.

There are also two major troughs in the data, lying to the left and right of the twin peaks of the mid-1990s. The first slow decline corresponds to the collapse of the ICA in the late-1980s, because the end of the ICA brought an end to the quotas growers were obliged to maintain in order to keep prices artificially high. Once the ICA had collapsed, coffee farmers everywhere were free to produce all the coffee they liked. The other large crater, the one lying to the right of the 1997 peak, reflects the entry of Vietnam into the coffee market. Even though Vietnam grows robusta beans and not arabicas, increasingly cheap robustas create downward pressure on arabica prices inasmuch as it is possible to substitute robustas for arabicas in blended coffees and instants. More recent upward price movements reflect some relative supply tightness near the end of the decade.

23

Beyond guaranteeing a minimum price for coffee, an FLO contract makes 60 percent of the funds available to the growers up front at the start of the growing season. This cash advance gives the growers needed start-up funds to pay for things such as supplies and fertilizers. It is interesting to compare this arrangement to the alternative arrangement between many small coffee growers and local buyers known as *coyotes*. A *coyote* is painted by the fair trade movement as an unscrupulous middleman who, because he may likely be the only available buyer for miles, gets away with paying cash for underpriced beans to poor coffee growers who have no other available buyers. In this case, it is the buyer who enjoys power through scarcity because growers' only choices are to sell to him or not.[11] While it is true that coyotes do try to pay the lowest price they can get, in many cases they also pay some or all of that money up front at the beginning of the growing season. Although the price per kilogram might be perceived as low, such an advance payment serves two important economic roles that benefit growers. First, the advance payment is a *loan*; coyotes lend their money for the duration of the growing season to farmers who would not be able to grow their crops otherwise. At the end of the season, the loan is paid back to the coyote in the form of coffee beans. Additionally, like any other loan, interest on the loan needs to be paid. In this instance, because the beans are the final payment, the initial loan must be smaller than the anticipated value of the crop in order to compensate the coyote for having to do without his money for several months. If the coyote's advance payment were equal to the value of the crop, that would amount to unjust treatment of the coyote.

The other important economic role served by the advance payment is that when a farmer strikes such a contract with a coyote at the beginning of the season, the farmer insulates himself from all risk for that year. Because the grower receives his money up front, he has no worries regarding what the going price of coffee will be at harvest time. That is now the exclusive problem of the coyote. In effect, by accepting a discounted amount of money from the coyote, the grower has purchased *insurance* against the future price of his coffee. The market value of the coffee at the end of the season is no longer of any concern to the farmer; it has become the coyote's worry.

At this point it is helpful to note one subtlety regarding the fair trade guaranteed prices. Fair trade entities like Max Havelaar and the Fairtrade Foundation make no price guarantees to individual growers, and no wage guarantees to workers. Instead, fair trade as it is practiced by the overseeing FLO makes a specific price guarantee only to organized cooperatives of producers—not to growers themselves. Further, wages paid to workers are not guaranteed to meet local minimum wage standards, and in some cases do not.[12]

FLO has a long-term strategy of gaining more Northern participants in the fair trade network: more importers, more roasters, and more distributors. There is no doubt that they have enjoyed some degree of success. There has even been a slow, gradual embrace of the idea by several MNCs. For example, after intense pressure, Starbucks is now the biggest buyer of fair trade coffee in North America, though it makes up less than 4 percent of the company's business.[13] Meanwhile, both Sara Lee, owner of the Douwe Egberts coffee brand, and Proctor and Gamble, who controls the Folgers and Millstone brands, now offer some fair trade coffees.[14] Nestlé has launched its own Partners' Blend of Nescafé, a fair trade certified instant coffee.[15]

Yet, according to Gavin Fridell, some of fair trade's greatest recent gains may be leaving a bitter taste in the mouths of many fair trade idealists: "Over the past two decades, the fair trade vision has changed ... to a market niche driven by the interests of giant conventional corporations with minor commitments to fair trade...."[16] In one case, the always enterprising Oaxacan growers of the UCIRI struck an exclusive deal with the French supermarket chain Carrefour to sell UCIRI coffee directly to Carrefour, to be sold under Carrefour's own fair trade certification label—altogether bypassing the oversight of the FLO. The FLO and its international partner organizations are especially wary of this new development and fearful that it could easily become a trend.[17]

Although Oxfam, a multinational group of nongovernmental organizations (NGOs) that fights global poverty and injustice, has been a key advocate for fair trade in the coffee industry, their primary desire is the eventual creation of a new ICA.[18] While current fair trade efforts are well-intentioned, Oxfam would argue, they are simply not serious enough nor comprehensive enough to do justice to the world's poor who grow coffee. Yet, Brink Lindsey argues that the fall of the original ICA led to fewer occasions for corruption along the coffee chain as consumers and producers grew closer along that chain, leading to *increases* in growers earnings rather than decreases.[19]

This chapter has briefly described the workings of the modern incarnation of fair trade, as well as summarized its predecessor, the International Coffee Agreement (ICA). The next chapter will evaluate the fair trade movement and consider carefully whether it can deliver on its promises to enrich the lives of the poor. Because this author is an economist, the chapter will also scrutinize the motives of each key player in the fair trade drama, including consumers, importers, retailers, and even the certifying organizations themselves. In all cases, the analysis will unpack whether the intentions of each actor are noble. If intentions do appear noble and genuine, then are the intended consequences of fair trade borne out? Or, are there unintended consequences—perhaps even consequences that do harm rather than good?

Notes

1 Gavin Fridell, *Fair Trade Coffee: The Prospects and Pitfalls of Market-Driven Social Justice* (Toronto: University of Toronto Press, 1997), 118–21.
2 Miriam Wasserman, "Trouble in Coffee Lands," Regional Review (Federal Reserve Bank of Boston) 12, no. 2 (2002): 9.
3 Pendergrast, *Uncommon Grounds*, 285.
4 Fridell, *Fair Trade Coffee*, 153.
5 Ibid., 110.
6 Ibid., 141.
7 Margaret Levi and April Linton, "Fair Trade: A Cup at a Time?" *Politics & Society* 31 (2003): 415.
8 Fridell, *Fair Trade Coffee*, 41–42.
9 Ibid., 53–54.
10 Ibid., 55.
11 Economists call this case of a single buyer a monopsony.
12 Jeremy Weber, "Fair Trade Coffee Enthusiasts Should Confront Reality," *Cato Journal* 27 (2007): 111. This issue will be considered again in the next chapter.
13 Weber, "Fair Trade Coffee Enthusiasts," 115.
14 Fridell, *Fair Trade Coffee*, 73.
15 *Economist*, "Voting with Your Trolley," December 7, 2006.
16 Fridell, *Fair Trade Coffee*, 6.
17 Ibid., 190.
18 Ibid., 145.
19 Brink Lindsey, "Grounds for Complaint? Understanding the 'Coffee Crisis,'" Trade Briefing Paper No. 16 (Washington, D.C.: Cato Institute, 2003), 8.

IV Can Fair Trade Work as Intended?

While the preceding chapter summarized briefly the modern fair trade movement, this section takes up the challenge of assessing the potential of fair trade to help the global poor relative to its claims. Clearly, consumers with kind hearts are paying more for their coffee, but does it make a difference?

What Else Is in a Cup of Fair Trade Coffee Besides Coffee?

Fair trade has caught on in part because it is perceived to be a market-oriented solution to the problem of extreme global poverty. Indeed one cannot make the argument that anyone is doing anything other than making independent choices in a global market. Fair trade advocates see paying higher prices for coffee as an act of compassion and justice—not as mere charity. No pro-trade organization such as the WTO can object to consumers voting freely with their dollars that a few cooperatives inside the fair trade network ought to receive more money for their product than other poor coffee growers do.

Unlike protectionist measures—such as the ICA's quotas—that kept prices artificially high, fair trade coffee prices are higher simply because consumers accept the idea that with a fair trade coffee purchase they find two goods in the cup: coffee and justice. Let us look more closely at each of these ideas: first, that fair trade is a bundle of two goods; and, second, that the invisible good in the cup is justice and not something else.

Leonardo Becchetti and Furio Camillo Rosati approach fair trade coffee from the bundling perspective, arguing that the primary marketing tool of fair trade is promoting awareness of consumers that there is indeed something beyond coffee in the cup. If fair trade marketing can convince consumers that selecting fair trade over other coffee is an act of personal social responsibility, then fair trade labeling will flourish. However, people will not pay a premium price for fair trade coffee for invisible justice unless marketing tells them it really does lie beneath the cup's rim.[1]

An alternative view of bundling is provided in two papers by Torsten Steinrücken and Sebastian Jaenichen. In their view, consumers are not buying justice or charity along with their coffee. The commodity they are willing to pay a bit extra for is the enhancement of their social reputation. Through simply incurring the pain of paying a higher price for coffee, one can appear as though one cares for the miserable plight of poor coffee growers, whether one actually does or not.[2] If others find this perceived quality admirable, then a social benefit may accrue to the consumer who buys fair trade coffee. Economists describe this as an investment in one's social capital; investing in one's reputation today leads to enhanced social opportunities in the future.

Thus, Steinrücken and Jaenichen see social capital for the buyer—not justice for the seller—as the product bundled together with the coffee found inside a fair trade certified bag of coffee. Beyond this assessment, still others argue that it is impossible to find justice inside a bag of coffee in the current fair trade arrangement. Although each pursues it along slightly different lines, two recent papers argue that justice is not a component of a fair trade purchase—which is quite different from what one hears in the rhetoric of fair trade advocates.

First, Malgorzata Kurjanska and Mathias Risse believe that any justice claims made by fair trade advocates are entirely unfounded, inasmuch as trade relations alone create no moral obligation by their mere existence. Because there is no wrongful harm being caused by any of the parties involved—after all, buying and selling happen only when trading is mutually beneficial to both parties—there is no wrong that demands to be corrected in the name of justice.[3]

Along related lines, Matthew Watson considers whether the fair trade purchases of consumers can be viewed as acts of justice using Adam Smith's concept of justice in his *Theory of Moral Sentiments* (*TMS*). Arguing from this Smithian perspective, Watson makes the case that while buying fair trade might perhaps be an act of virtue, it does not amount to an act of justice. First, Watson argues that—at least for Adam Smith—moral human actions rise to the level of acts of justice only when there is a specific wrong or harm that requires neutralizing. Thus, like Kurjanska and Risse, Watson does not see buying fair trade as an act of justice, inasmuch as there is nothing inhumane about buying goods from someone selling them at a price the seller willingly accepts. This is not to say that buying fair trade is bereft of kindness; indeed, the entire fair trade movement rests on the willingness of consumers to pay a little extra for their coffee in the belief that they are helping the poor. Watson merely argues that Adam Smith would see the purchases fair trade buyers make as virtuous acts of beneficence, rather than as virtuous acts of justice.[4]

Moreover, the modern practice of fair trade omits one of the key motives for human behavior found in Smith's *TMS*: a longing for mutual sympathy of feeling. When distant Northern consumers buy coffee grown by poor farmers the consumers do not know, those consumers cannot genuinely share the feelings of the coffee growers—either their past miseries or their joy at receiving the higher price for their coffee that fair trade brings. Smith's writing is at its most beautiful and tender in describing the ways in which one person can lighten another's burden through a genuine sympathy of feeling:

> How are the unfortunate relieved when they have found out a person to whom they can communicate the cause of their sorrow? Upon his sympathy they seem to disburden themselves of a part of their distress: he is not improperly said to share it with them. He not only feels a sorrow of the same kind with that which they feel, but as if he had derived a part of it to himself, what he feels seems to alleviate the weight of what they feel. Yet by relating their misfortunes they in some measure renew their grief. They awaken in their memory the remembrance of those circumstances which occasioned their affliction. Their tears accordingly flow faster than before, and they are apt to abandon themselves to all the weakness of sorrow. They take pleasure, however, in all this, and, it is evident, are sensibly relieved by it; because the sweetness of his sympathy more than compensates the bitterness of that sorrow, which, in order to excite this sympathy, they had thus enlivened and renewed.[5]

Yet, in the modern fair trade coffee movement, consumers and growers are simply not connected other than through a for-profit middleman (such as Equal Exchange). In addition, according to Gavin Fridell, the disconnect between consumers and growers is increasingly large:

> While fair trade is premised on the notion of bringing Southern producers and Northern consumers into direct relations with each other, in reality the direct relations that are formed in the fair trade network are primarily between Southern producers and Northern ATOs [alternative trade organizations], with the links to actual consumers still mediated by the market. Moreover, ... face-to-face visits from Northern consumer groups to Southern cooperatives have declined.[6]

Fair Trade as a Marketing Strategy

Given that at least some consumers are clearly prepared to pay a bit extra for coffee that they believe is served with a splash of justice in the cup, it seems legitimate to ask whether fair trade coffee arrangements are thinly disguised attempts to charge morally concerned customers higher prices for a cup of coffee than the less concerned among us are willing to pay. It really is an excellent question to ask because firms are always seeking ways to charge each of their customers the highest price he or she will pay.

In most of our market interactions, we consumers all pay the same price for the same good. Shopkeepers charge all of us the same prices for a gallon of milk, a loaf of bread, or a jar of peanut butter. For every purchase we voluntarily make, we find we are better off having bought the good. When we buy milk, we value the milk more than we valued the dollars we willingly handed over, and the shopkeeper is eager to trade the milk for our dollars. Now, we consumers might wish we could pay even less, and the shopkeeper might wish he could charge even more, but in most instances all exchanges are made at the going rate—the price at which the quantity of milk demanded by consumers exactly matches the amount of milk sellers are willing to make available. As further evidence that both buyer and seller are enriched by such voluntary exchanges, we normally hear each say, "Thank you," at the conclusion of the transaction.

Although consumers in most markets pay the same price, we consumers differ in terms of the maximum price we would each be willing to pay for some good or service. The shopkeepers we encounter would dearly love to know the maximum price each of us would pay for each good in our baskets. Imagine, if you will, an enchanted store—well, enchanted from the seller's perspective—in which the monetary value each customer places on a gallon of milk is visible, only to the seller, in a large-sized font on each customer's forehead. Rather than charge all of us the same price, the seller would instead happily charge each of us a price quite close to each value being secretly revealed to him. In doing so, he would find even more cash in his till at the close of the day.

While we do not actually have numbers on our foreheads that give away our willingness to buy a certain good or service, sellers in many cases are nevertheless able to get us to reveal some information about ourselves that gives away either our ability to pay or our desire for the product. For example, students are charged less for movie tickets than the rest of us. Senior citizens receive a senior discount for meals, while the rest of us pay the full menu price. Nearly all of us are charged more for a phone call during a weekday than on the weekend.

In all three of these examples, some of us pay higher prices because we give ourselves away to sellers. In the case of student discounts, those of us who do not possess student ID cards are probably not on student budgets, and thus pay the higher price. In restaurants, those of us with younger-looking skin—and hair that is not yet gray[7]—are probably not yet retired and living on fixed incomes, and thus we are charged more than our silver-haired elders. Because a telephone call placed during a working day is probably more urgent than one made on a Saturday afternoon, phone companies charge us more for the weekday call.

Sellers' use of clues that we ourselves reveal to them regarding our willingness to pay is called price discrimination.[8] We use the word *discrimination* because people are being charged different prices for the same goods and services: Different consumers are being treated differently, even though everyone buys the same product.

In his book *The Undercover Economist*, columnist Tim Harford shares the remarkable case of Costa Coffee's fair trade coffee pricing. Before Mr. Harford began poking his investigative nose into Costa Coffee's pricing, Costa charged its customers in the United Kingdom ten pence more (about 18 cents) for a fair trade cappuccino. Many concerned customers willingly paid the higher price for a cup that came along with the assurance that through their purchase they were doing good.

According to Harford, Costa purchased its fair trade coffee from Cafédirect, a leading fair trade brand in the United Kingdom. Now, Cafédirect paid fair trade growers a premium of between 40 and 55 pence (up to one dollar) per pound of coffee—an amount large enough to change significantly a farmer's standard of living. Yet, because a cappuccino requires a mere quarter-ounce of coffee per cup, using fair trade coffee to make cappuccinos should lead to an increase in Costa's costs of less than one cent per cup. Nevertheless, Costa was charging nearly twenty times that premium.

In this case, about 17 cents per cappuccino was going missing between the Costa counter and the coffee grower. It is possible that Cafédirect and Costa were miserably inefficient companies that were simply losing the 17 cents along the way, but it is also possible that Costa was pocketing it as profit. After Mr. Harford drew this discrepancy to Costa's attention, "Costa worked out that the whole business gave the wrong impression, and at the end of 2004 began to offer fair trade coffee on request, *without* a price premium. Costa abandoned the premium of fair trade coffee because it was bad public relations, not because it was unprofitable."[9] This begs the question of why it had been profitable for Costa to charge higher prices for fair trade cappuccinos. The answer lies in price discrimination. It turns out that caring people will pay higher prices for coffee when they believe buying it helps others. Mr. Harford continues:

> … fair trade coffee allowed Costa to find customers who are willing to pay a bit more if given a reason to do so. By ordering a fair trade cappuccino, you sent two messages to Costa. One message interested them very little:
> "I think that fair trade coffee is a product that should be supported."
> The second message is the one that they were straining to hear: "I don't really mind paying a bit extra."[10]

It should come as no great surprise, then, that a considerable academic literature has evolved investigating fair trade coffee prices as price discrimination, by viewing fair trade coffee as a strategy to get "ethical" consumers to hand over more of their money. Socially conscious consumers self-identify by selecting certified fair trade coffees over other coffees, a behavior that is immensely helpful to coffee sellers.

In one study, Chris Arnot, Peter Boxall, and Sean Cash investigated the price sensitivity of the demand for fair trade coffee. That is—using a term we discussed earlier—these authors estimated the price elasticity of the demand for fair trade coffee. Just how quickly are buyers scared away from buying fair trade as its price rises?

Their experiment was ingeniously simple. Once they found a coffee vendor on a university campus willing to help, they varied the price of two medium roast coffees—one that was fair trade and one that was not—several times over the course of the study. By changing the price of the fair trade coffee relative to the price of the other, they were able to observe precisely how quickly consumers abandoned fair trade coffee as its price rose in relation to the price of the other coffee. The results suggested that those who buy fair trade, and are motivated out of concern, are almost entirely insensitive to price increases. They will generally order fair trade, even if the price of fair trade rises or if the price of the standard coffee goes on sale.[11] Thus, while the demand for all coffee is quite price inelastic (as noted above), the demand for fair trade coffee is even more so. The coffee retailer in the study could easily increase total revenues by raising the price of the fair trade coffee. The vendor would no doubt lose some fair trade sales, but he would not lose very many. A modest increase in the price of the remaining sales would more than make up for the few sales lost.

Other studies have attempted to identify some basic demographics of the consumers sufficiently concerned to pay a bit extra for fair trade coffee and also to identify the price point at which even they might decide fair trade is too expensive. Arnot, Boxall, and Cash found that university students were less price sensitive to increases in fair trade coffee relative to nonfair trade than were staff and faculty at the same university.[12] This result is consistent with the findings of Leonardo Becchetti and Furio Camillo Rosati who collected demographic data about shoppers who frequent shops specializing in fair trade products. These customers were found to be 32 percent students, 26 percent retirees, 12 percent housewives, and 8 percent professionals; twice as many females as males frequented such shops.[13]

In the *Journal of Consumer Affairs*, Patrick De Pelsmacker, Liesbeth Driesen, and Glenn Rayp go a step further and divide the coffee drinkers they studied at Belgium's University of Ghent into four mutually-exclusive classes. Fair Trade Lovers are those for whom fair trade is the most important attribute of coffee, and they comprise 11 percent of the market considered in the study. Fair Trade Likers make up 40 percent of the market, and they are motivated by fair trade but care about other attributes like taste and brand more than the Fair Trade Lovers do. Flavor Lovers make up 24 percent of buyers, and Brand Lovers constitute the remaining 25 percent.[14] The authors find that, of the subjects studied, only about 10 percent of all coffee drinkers are willing to pay the existing Belgian fair trade premium of 27 percent[15] and that the average premium people are willing to pay was just 10 percent.[16] Thus, it appears that the demand for fair trade coffee is price inelastic within some reasonable range, but even the most concerned among us will abandon it at some point as the price rises. Torsten Steinrücken and Sebastian Jaenichen provide a nice summary of an existing literature suggesting that ethical behavior is most likely to be observed in situations of relatively low cost.[17] Or, in Gavin Fridell's words, fair trade prices "cannot be so high as to scare off 'ethical consumers' in the North."[18]

As the discussion thus far in this chapter suggests, fair trade branding might in part be a marvelous way to induce concerned people everywhere to spend more on their coffee than they otherwise would. Gavin Fridell suggests fair trade branding bears a resemblance to Juan Valdez: both are marketing and/or labeling strategies that target specific market segments.[19]

At this point it is important to note that fair trade organizations guarantee only the minimum price that will be received by the growers. They make no such guarantee that you will receive a reasonable price at the point of purchase. When it comes to the price that will be paid by consumers, fair trade coffee vendors are most likely just like any other coffee vendors: They try to get you to pay the highest possible price that will also cover their costs. One way to do that is to suggest or imply that the aid you make available to the poor when you buy fair trade is directly proportional to the hefty markup on that cup of coffee you are buying.

Price discrimination may not be the only marketing tool at work in the fair trade coffee market. While price discrimination keeps revenues high for companies such as Costa, Equal Exchange, and even your neighborhood coffee bar, firms of all kinds do better when they can keep their costs low. Fair trade roasters like Equal Exchange benefit when they can find ways to reduce costs such as advertising and distribution.

This may very well be the why Equal Exchange has worked to gain a monopoly over mainline protestants' coffee concessions. Through its Interfaith Program, Equal Exchange now commands a hefty share of the caring-coffee-drinker market. The Interfaith Program has official partnerships with at least a dozen large faith groups. The Interfaith Program is not restricted to any particular creed; its partnerships include the American Jewish World Service Fair Trade Project and the Islamic Relief USA Fair Trade Project.

In this author's past place of worship, dedicated parishioners freely gave of their time and talents throughout the year to serve the retailing, advertising, and distribution efforts of Equal Exchange. Those parishioners who had taken on the ministry of fair trade coffee advertised frequently in the weekly bulletin and monthly newsletter—at no charge, of course. They also operated a coffee cart that was open for business between and after Sunday services, and they took great care to stock up on extra-special goodies in anticipation of gift-giving occasions such as Christmas and Valentine's Day. They carefully maintained their inventory on hand, placing orders with Equal Exchange when stocks were getting low. Of course, Equal Exchange was the only coffee served during coffee hour, where an Equal Exchange sign was prominently displayed to remind everyone that ours was a congregation that cared about the poor.

This author knows that his brothers and sisters in Christ were thinking only of the poor as they worked in the service of the congregation's fair trade coffee ministry. This author is also quite certain that Equal Exchange was delighted that our church served as one more retail outlet selling their product— not to mention one that was giving them much free publicity and even providing free weekly tastings during the postworship fellowship. In any other setting but a church, the message would be clear: If you enjoyed today's free sample, be sure to pick some up on your way out to savor at home all week long.

Bottom Line: Does Fair Trade Coffee Help the Poor?

While it may be fair to cast doubt on the purity of the motives of sellers of fair trade branded coffee and also to ask whether buying fair trade is indeed an act of justice rather than mere charity, such questions do not address the most fundamental questions of all. First, does fair trade coffee enrich the lives of the poor coffee growers the movement claims to help? Second, if fair trade does make a difference, is that difference one that is just palliative, merely making life a bit less onerous for a few of the world's poor? Or can fair trade lead to genuinely transformational, lasting change?

Even if fair trade is a viable antipoverty strategy—and later in this section we will evaluate such claims—it is not a very big one. Fair trade coffee roughly represents just 1 percent of the coffee markets in the United States and Europe.[20] In 2000, fair trade occupied 3 percent of the Swiss market, 2.7 percent in the Netherlands, 1.8 percent in Denmark, 1.5 percent in the

United Kingdom, and less than 1 percent elsewhere. In fact, even though fair trade coffee demand has risen steadily over the past fifteen years, Gavin Fridell believes that northern fair trade coffee markets may already be saturated, noting that fair trade cooperatives can sell just 10–30 percent of their fair trade coffee in the fair trade market; faced with no other option, they sell off the remainder of their crop in the conventional coffee market at the prevailing price.[21] Torsten Steinrücken and Sebastian Jaenichen are slightly more optimistic, noting that in 2002 fair trade growers sold something between 25 and 50 percent of their harvest at fair trade prices: They sold off the rest at the market-determined so-called unfair prices.[22]

Thus, while there is too much coffee being grown relative to global demand in general, there is also not sufficient demand to purchase, at the fair trade price, all of the coffee being grown as fair trade coffee. In both cases, there is simply too much coffee. In an effort to bolster the efforts of FLO's certifying organizations, the governments of five European nations—Belgium, Denmark, France, Switzerland, and the Netherlands (the home of Max Havelaar)—all subsidize the fair trade effort.[23] In these five instances, the free-market portrayal of the fair trade movement falls a bit flat.

Let us examine more closely the consequences—both intended and unintended—of the fair trade coffee movement. Russ Roberts, professor of economics and the J. Fish and Lillian F. Smith Distinguished Scholar at the Mercatus Center at George Mason University, compares the premium price that we voluntarily pay to help out poor coffee growers to a hypothetical "tip jar" at a place like Wal-Mart.[24] According to an anti-Wal-Mart organization, in 2008 the average full time Wal-Mart Associate (34 hours per week) earned $10.84 per hour.[25] Although that hourly wage rate lies well above the current minimum wage, if a family tried to live on only that income, it would have an extremely difficult time: It amounts to just $19,165, which lies $2,000 below the federal poverty line for a family of four.

In Roberts's metaphor, we consumers feel bad—and justifiably so—that Wal-Mart associates have a difficult time making ends meet. Thus, caring members of our society work very hard to see that tip jars are placed at each cash register in each Wal-Mart, each with a sign that reads:

> Your cashier and other employees here
> make less than the average wage
> in the United States.
> Please help them out.

Of course consumers of all kinds, including many who are poor and working-class themselves, and perhaps who earn even less than $10.84 per hour, frequent Wal-Mart. Suppose, though, that the tip jar turns out to be an effective way to raise the pay of Wal-Mart's workers—assuming that we could all get over the condescending and potentially dehumanizing impact that such a jar might bring with it. Suppose further that the jar works really well—so well that it raises the average wage of a Wal-Mart employee from $10.84 to $13.84 per hour. What might happen as a result?

While many of us might look at this result and say to ourselves, "How nice. The poor Wal-Mart workers are now making more money," an economist looks at this outcome and sees something else. What immediately grabs the economist's attention is the fact that the effective hourly wage of working at Wal-Mart just went up by three bucks an hour. It really does not matter where the money came from: Working at Wal-Mart now pays nearly 30 percent better than it used to. Seeing this, the economist can make some fairly sensible predictions regarding how different actors in this unfolding economic drama will behave now that the incentive arrangements have changed.

One of the fundamental truths of economics—and one that University of Chicago economist Steven Levitt reminds us in his bestselling book *Freakonomics*—is that incentives matter. Once the stakes of any economic game have changed, people alter their behaviors accordingly. Economists assume so because they believe that people are rational, at least on average. Hence, we may reasonably anticipate that when an opportunity for improving one's lot presents itself, it would be irrational not to alter one's behavior in response. Economist and funnyman Yoram Bauman humorously simplifies this rationality assumption as, "People are stupid, but people aren't *that* stupid."

What an economist sees in the tip-jar metaphor is simply this: Working at Wal-Mart now looks three dollars per hour more attractive than it did before the tip jars appeared. Bear in mind also that the Wal-Mart associates who willingly worked at Wal-Mart for $10.84 per hour were choosing to do so because that represented their best available option. If they had better offers available, presumably they should have taken them already. Now that the hourly average at Wal-Mart looks three dollars an hour better than it used to, people not currently working at Wal-Mart, but currently earning something between $10.84 and $13.84, will begin filling out applications to work at Wal-Mart. Further, these new applicants on average will be stronger applicants than those individuals who were already working at Wal-Mart. We have a good idea that this is true because until the tip jar arrived on the scene, they were making more money than the average Wal-Mart associate.

Over time, slowly but surely, the less-experienced and less-skilled Wal-Mart employees will be replaced at Wal-Mart by better-qualified applicants who now are attracted to Wal-Mart by its higher wages. Mike Munger, chair of the Department of Political Science at Duke University, calls this phenomenon "job gentrification."[26] As with urban gentrification, in which the relatively affluent move into historically poor urban neighborhoods, thereby raising housing prices so that the poor can no longer afford to live there, in this case better qualified and more experienced applicants will move in and take the jobs of those who enjoy fewer competitive advantages in the labor market.

Despite these unintended negative consequences of the tip jar, the compassionate activists who worked hard for the institution of the tip jar in the first place might nevertheless claim victory. After all, working at Wal-Mart now pays better than it used to. Indeed, some people are now making more money than they used to. If the tip-jar advocates look more closely, however, they will discover that the faces have changed, and that by effectively raising the wage they created incentives for outsiders to supply even more labor for Wal-Mart in a market where the wages are low because there are already too many people who possess the minimum skill set necessary to ably perform the job. The poor Wal-Mart workers that the well-intentioned tip-jar advocates thought they were helping have now been displaced from the very jobs that had been their best available option.

Although the pay is dramatically lower, growing coffee in our global economy is a lot like working at Wal-Mart in our domestic economy. Both occupations are noble. Good, decent, hard-working people daily put forward their best efforts as they seek to make life better for themselves and their families. In both cases, however, wages are relatively low: Many people can perform the tasks required because few skills are needed. If growing coffee is like working at Wal-Mart, then buying fair trade coffee is like putting a few dollars in the Wal-Mart tip jar.

In the same way that voluntarily raising Wal-Mart's wages by paying a bit extra would increase the number of people interested in working at Wal-Mart, voluntarily raising the prices paid to coffee growers has lead to an unanticipated surge in the number of coffee growers seeking to enter fair trade agreements, making it extremely difficult for growers to enter the fair trade network. Competition for fair trade contracts has grown extremely stiff, so much so that getting a spot on the FLO's register of cooperatives has become almost impossible.[27] One Mexican cooperative searched for eight years to find a willing buyer.[28]

If the fundamental problem with the coffee market is that prices are low because there is too much coffee, then it would appear that the fair trade movement may be making matters worse rather than better because it increases the incentives to grow more coffee. As early as 2001, the FLO stated that it was reluctant to register any additional coffee cooperatives.[29] In 2002, the FLO temporarily closed its registry, thereby shutting out most of the world's poorest coffee growers.[30] Even Trent University's Gavin Fridell, who is no fan of the free market, writes: "In the South, indications of growing competition have emerged between established fair trade cooperatives, newer fair trade cooperatives, and non-certified cooperatives as they battle for a share of the stagnating fair trade coffee market."[31]

To compound matters, it appears that the sorts of caring customers prepared to purchase fair trade coffee are motivated by other causes as well. Just like the concerned among us will pay a bit extra if our coffee has been fair trade certified, evidence suggests we are also willing to pay a premium for coffee that is certified as organic, or certified as "shade-grown" (i.e., bird friendly). Thus, when caring consumers face multiple options such as these in the marketplace, then fair trade coffee has the unenviable task of competing with the organic and shade-grown coffees for shares of the available buyers in the concerned-coffee-buyer segment.[32]

As we evaluate the effectiveness of fair trade coffee as an antipoverty strategy, we should ask just how great an impact our paying a bit extra for our coffee has upon the lives of the growers we intend to help. This question is especially interesting because we never actually see the people we are presumably helping. At least in the case of the Wal-Mart tip jar we know that every dollar we chip in goes directly to the workers we hope to assist. That is also exactly how it works at your local coffee bar; each dollar you put in the tip jar goes directly to your able barista. However, the fair trade arrangement lacks such utter transparency. All we know is that we have paid a higher price for our coffee and that someone has promised that some of that money will get to coffee growers: not all of it, as we have already seen, but at least some of it.

As mentioned earlier, very little of the price you pay for a cup of coffee at a coffee bar is actually for coffee; depending on your beverage, the cost of the coffee is just 5 to 7 percent of the retail price of the drink. Given that we all pay a large premium for coffee—whether fair trade or not—it is reasonable to wonder just how much good we are actually accomplishing.

According to Torsten Steinrücken and Sebastian Jaenichen, there is still very little quality data regarding precisely what fraction of the fair trade coffee retail price travels all the way backward along the supply chain to the growers themselves. The consensus view, even if informed mostly by anecdotal evidence thus far, is that overhead costs are high.[33] While one study claims that the higher prices of fair trade coffee generally go toward (1) financing the regulatory structure of the FLO and its member organizations, and (2) higher pay for an association's growers,[34] there is increasing evidence that there may be a mismatch between consumers' expectations and the realities of life inside a fair trade cooperative. Writing for the *Financial Times*, Hal Weitzman found that fair trade workers were being paid less than the local minimum wage.[35] In a series of articles from his trip, Weitzman describes several other troubling accounts that call into question whether coffee bearing the fair trade label was actually produced under the FLO's guaranteed conditions. Weitzman relates conversations with insiders working in the industry who revealed that nonfair trade coffee was being fraudulently sold as fair trade coffee and also that fair trade coffees have been planted "in protected national rainforest land in the northern Peruvian jungle."[36] Even the UCIRI, those entrepreneurial coffee growers from Oaxaca who were instrumental in creating Max Havelaar as the first fair trade brand, have grown increasingly frustrated with the FLO. UCIRI members feel as if they have little say over either the FLO's operations or the criteria it chooses to use in either the certification process or the admission of new entrants to the FLO's register of cooperatives.

The discussion so far leads to two discouraging conclusions. First, as Paul Collier notes in his bestselling book *The Bottom Billion*, fair trade is simply charity: "The price premium in fair trade products is a form of charitable transfer...."[37] Second, if fair trade indeed bundles coffee with charity as Torsten Steinrücken and Sebastian Jaenichen have suggested, "there are more efficient mechanisms of redistribution than the rather expensive fair trade concept."[38] Even if fair trade does some good, it may not be much. These conclusions are what lead Philip Booth and Linda Whetstone to suggest that it may be equally ethical and far more effective in enriching the poor to simply "buy Maxwell House coffee and pay the equivalent of the fair trade premium to a charitable cause."[39]

Notes

[1] Leonardo Becchetti and Furio Camillo Rosati, "Global Social Preferences and the Demand for Socially Responsible Products: Empirical Evidence from a Pilot Study on Fair Trade Consumers," *The World Economy* 30 (2007): 810.

[2] Torsten Steinrücken and Sebastian Jaenichen, "The Fair Trade Idea: Towards an Economics of Social Labels," *Journal of Consumer Policy* 30 (2007): 205. See also Torsten Steinrücken and Sebastian Jaenichen, "Does the Fair Trade Concept Work? An Economic Analysis of Social Labels," *Aussenwirtschaft* 61, no. 2 (2006): 189–210.

[3] Malgorzata Kurjanska and Mathias Risse, "Fairness in Trade II: Export Subsidies and the Fair Trade Movement," *Politics, Philosophy, & Economics* 7 (2008): 44.

[4] Matthew Watson, "Trade Justice and Individual Consumption Choices: Adam Smith's Spectator Theory and the Moral Constitution of the Fair Trade Consumer," *European Journal of International Relations* 13 (2007): 265.

[5] Adam Smith, *The Theory of Moral Sentiments*, ed. D. D. Raphael and A. L. Macfie, vol. 1, Glasgow Edition of the Works and Correspondence of Adam Smith (Indianapolis, Ind.: Liberty Fund, 1982), 15.

[6] Gavin Fridell, *Fair Trade Coffee: The Prospects and Pitfalls of Market-Driven Social Justice* (Toronto: University of Toronto Press, 1997), 194.

[7] While this silver-haired author is just forty-six years old at the time of publication, he has nevertheless been granted the lower senior-citizen price for a cup of coffee on at least one occasion.

[8] This specific form of price discrimination—breaking the market into a few specific customer segments—is called third-degree price discrimination. Second-degree price discrimination comes in the form of a quantity discount, and first-degree price discrimination is the theoretical possibility that each consumer is charged a price exactly equal to the maximum price

he is willing to pay. Car salesmen work very hard negotiating with each individual customer in an effort to get close to this outcome.

9 Tim Harford, *The Undercover Economist* (Oxford, U.K.: Oxford University Press, 2006), 33.

10 Ibid., 34.

11 Chris Arnot, Peter C. Boxall, and Sean B. Cash, "Do Ethical Consumers Care About Price? A Revealed Preference Analysis of Fair Trade Coffee Purchases," *Canadian Journal of Agricultural Economics* 54 (2006): 557, 563.

12 Ibid., 559.

13 Becchetti and Rosati, "Global Social Preferences," 813.

14 Patrick De Pelsmacker, Liesbeth Driesen, and Glenn Rayp, "Do Consumers Care about Ethics? Willingness to Pay for Fair-Trade Coffee," *Journal of Consumer Affairs* 39 (2005): 363.

15 Ibid., 381.

16 Ibid., 376.

17 Steinrücken and Jaenichen, "The Fair Trade Idea," 206.

18 Fridell, *Fair Trade Coffee*, 56.

19 Ibid., 169.

20 Miriam Wasserman, "Trouble in Coffee Lands," *Regional Review* (Federal Reserve Bank of Boston) 12, no. 2 (2002): 10.

21 Fridell, *Fair Trade Coffee*, 64, 188.

22 Steinrücken and Jaenichen, "The Fair Trade Idea," 210.

23 Margaret Levi and April Linton, "Fair Trade: A Cup at a Time?" *Politics & Society* 31 (2003): 419.

24 Mike Munger, "Munger on Fair Trade and Free Trade: Interview with Russ Roberts," *EconTalk*, December 3, 2007, http://www.econtalk.org/archives/2007/12/munger_on_fair.html.

25 See http://wakeupwalmart.com/facts/.

26 Munger, "Munger on Fair Trade."

27 Fridell, *Fair Trade Coffee*, 98.

28 Ibid., 219–20.

29 Ibid., 69.

30 Jeremy Weber, "Fair Trade Coffee Enthusiasts Should Confront Reality," *Cato Journal* 27 (2007): 112.

31 Fridell, *Fair Trade Coffee*, 281.

32 Ibid., 78.

33 Steinrücken and Jaenichen, "The Fair Trade Idea," 208–9.

34 De Pelsmacker, Driesen, and Rayp, "Do Consumers Care about Ethics?" 367.

35 Hal Weitzman, "Bitter Cost of 'Fair Trade' Coffee: An *FT* Investigation Finds Premium Price Beans Are Picked by Workers Paid Below Minimum Wage," *Financial Times* (September 9, 2006).

[36] Hal Weitzman, "'Ethical-Coffee' Workers Paid Below Legal Minimum," *Financial Times* (September 9, 2006).

[37] Paul Collier, *The Bottom Billion: Why the Poorest Countries Are Failing and What Can Be Done About It* (Oxford, UK: Oxford University Press, 2007), 163.

[38] Steinrücken and Jaenichen, "The Fair Trade Idea," 216.

[39] Philip Booth and Linda Whetstone, "Half a Cheer for Fair Trade," *Economic Affairs* 27, no. 2 (2007): 31.

V How Might a Caring Christian Respond?

When Jesus was anointed at Bethany, he reminded us of what is written in Deuteronomy 15:11: "There will always be poor people in the land. Therefore I command you to be openhanded toward your brothers and toward the poor and needy in your land."[1] In Matthew 25:40, he tells us that when we serve the poor we also serve him. Through both word and example, Christ calls us to care for the poor and also to welcome them as we would welcome our Master.

Given the extent of poverty in the world today and its miserable depths in some nations, surely we are called to be agents for change on their behalf. Even though we can never personally know every person who may be most pressed by economic circumstances, we must nevertheless serve him. We cannot serve our Master directly, but we serve him when we come to the aid of others.

Our response must be thoughtful, careful, and prayerful. Surely we do not want to serve our Master in some slapdash, haphazard effort. This requires responding to urgent needs both with speed and with an understanding of what is needed most. Too often we simply throw things at a problem—because we do indeed have much to give—rather than find out first what is needed most and where we can serve most effectively. When needs are persistent rather than temporary, we must stay focused on our hope for the long-term improvement of the prospects of the subjects of our care. Just as we must treat others as we would treat our Lord, sometimes it is helpful to ask ourselves what we would do if a specific individual we already know and care for were in similar circumstances.

The modern fair trade movement has marvelous intentions. This author has dear friends who are also dedicated brothers and sisters in the faith who believe they are saving the world by purchasing Equal Exchange's coffees and chocolate or by staffing the Equal Exchange coffee concession between church services. They carry out those duties with joy, love, good humor, and the belief that they are agents for change acting on behalf of the "least of these."

Yet, the fair trade movement, for all its good intentions, cannot deliver on what it promises. Simply put, coffee growers are poor because there is too much coffee. Fair trade simply does not address that fundamental reality. In fact, by guaranteeing a price to growers that is higher than the world price of coffee, fair trade makes the supply of coffee even larger than it would otherwise be. As we have already seen, whenever coffee prices increase, there will be another coffee grower, and another, and another.

There is no question that *some* people benefit from the fair trade movement. Beginning in your neighborhood and moving outward, your local coffee bar benefits, as does Equal Exchange or some other fair trade company that supplies your coffee shop. Fair Trade USA benefits by charging aspiring cooperatives an entrance fee, and Fair Trade USA benefits by charging companies such as Equal Exchange for use of their fair trade mark—the primary source of Fair Trade USA's income. Of the extra dollar or two that you pay for a bag of coffee, at least some tiny part remains by the time it travels all the way back through the entire supply chain to the needy growers you are seeking to serve.[2] At least we hope so. Kate Bird and David Hughes state that "… due to lack of data and the low volumes of coffee exported using fair trade marketing systems, a causal relationship between fair trade and enhanced producer welfare cannot be proved categorically."[3]

Further, because we know little if anything about the people we attempt to help through fair trade—the actual individuals who have names and faces—it is nearly impossible for each of us to know whether or not we are righting some past wrong or correcting some harm. We certainly know little if anything at all about what a given country's best long-term development strategy might be. Perhaps the best face that may be put on the realities of fair trade is one provided by Malgorzata Kurjanska and Mathias Risse:

> … a difficulty arises when consumers cannot distinguish between situations in which they ought to buy Fair Trade and when they ought not to do so. What, then, ought one to do? … From a first-person standpoint, we can resolve this situation by noting that Fair Trade does not occupy large market shares…. So even if supporting particular producers is not a good development strategy, the potential harm is minimal…. [O]ne does little harm while benefitting *somebody* immediately…. [P]ermissibility to purchase Fair Trade products hinges on the movement's improbability of hindering more feasible development strategies. This might be less force than defenders of the Fair Trade movement might hope for, but it is hard to see how to make their case stronger.[4]

The Promise of Free Trade

Despite its marvelous intentions, as well as the good-faith monetary contributions that consumers make when they choose higher-priced fair trade coffee over other coffee, fair trade will never lead to the long-term enrichment of the poor. Instead, it creates an additional incentive for the poor to continue to soldier on in a line of work that will never pay much better than it does right now. As long as coffee prices remain low, growing coffee—even if it is fair trade coffee—will not pay well. The reason that coffee prices remain low is because there is too much of it. The fair trade movement does no favors for the poor by encouraging even more poor people to grow even more coffee, but that is precisely the effect that a higher fair trade price is having, leading to the FLO's reluctance to take on any more cooperatives.

Low coffee prices, like low prices for any other commodity, normally are a signal to producers to make less of it and move onto something else instead. Yet, fair trade frustrates this signal, with unfortunate consequences. First, fair trade encourages even more coffee production. Second, fair trade makes non-fair trade growers poorer because non-fair trade prices fall as new growers in places such as Vietnam are attracted into the market by artificially high prices.[5] Entry by new growers increases the supply, and bigger supplies of anything drive prices downward.

Another unintended consequence of fair trade agreements is that they weaken the incentives of coffee growers to increase the market appeal of their beans through quality improvements, or to reduce their production costs through improved techniques. Unlike Colombia, a nation that improved demand for its coffee by focusing on its quality, fair trade growers have little incentive to do likewise.[6] This is especially distressing because all market research regarding fair trade agrees that coffee quality nearly always trumps fair trade for consumers as a reason to pay a higher price, even among the Fair Trade Lovers described earlier.[7] Generally speaking, coffee drinkers buy first on quality.[8]

Thus, fair trade agreements act like golden handcuffs that bind the wrists of fair trade cooperatives and their member growers. Fair trade discourages member growers from trying something new that they would certainly otherwise try if they did not have the security of the fair trade price.[9] As John

Wilkinson puts it, "North-South Fair Trade ... could never itself be a sufficient strategy for rural development," reminding us that fair trade coffee accounts for only 20 percent of all coffee sold by fair trade cooperatives. Further, while there are about five hundred groups worldwide in forty-nine countries, this implies that we are talking about an average of just ten groups per country.[10]

The moral shortcoming of the fair trade movement is that it keeps the poor shackled to activities that, while productive, will never lead to poverty reduction on a large scale—or even a modest one. Further, if our purchases of fair trade really do retard the long-term rate of poverty reduction, then buying fair trade might rightly be viewed as causing harm.[11]

As a case for comparison, Malgorzata Kurjanska and Mathias Risse point to Costa Rica. Costa Rica has shifted its production of goods away from traditional fair trade products such as bananas and coffee, and toward new exports and ecotourism. As a result, Costa Rica's exports of nontraditional goods rose from just 38.6 percent in 1982 to 87.0 percent by 2003. Fair trade loving northern consumers, despite their good intentions, would have resisted such a shift in production. Yet, the shift is one that over time has led to conditions even better than those that fair trade alone could deliver.[12]

When the price of something is low, like coffee, market forces normally direct people to make less of it and move onto something else, but fair trade interferes with the signal that prices ordinarily provide; it can never serve as a sustainable long-term development strategy. Paul Collier, a former World Bank director of development research puts it this way in his bestselling *The Bottom Billion*:

> The price premium in fair trade products is a form of charitable transfer, and there is evidently no harm in that. But the problem with it, as compared with just giving people the aid in other ways, is that it encourages recipients to stay doing what they are doing—producing coffee. A key economic problem for the bottom billion

is that producers have not diversified out of a narrow range of primary commodities. Raising their prices (albeit infinitesimally, since fair trade is such a small component of demand) makes it harder for people to move into other activities. They get charity as long as they stay producing the crops that have locked them into poverty.[13]

Tim Harford echoes Collier, observing that coffee farmers will never be rich until everyone else is first; that is, until coffee growing becomes rare enough that it can command a higher price. Because fair trade creates more coffee, and not less, coffee will never pay well. Thus, only long-term growth and development will help the poor grow rich.[14]

What, then, can lead to real and lasting economic gains for the poor? The good news is that we have considerable information about this question, and a rich feast of evidence confirming the answer that economics provides. When prices are free to act as a signal showing people what to make either more or less of, poor people begin to flourish. For example, even though there continues to be income inequality within nations, inequality across the entire globe has *decreased* over the last quarter century. More importantly, the rate of extreme poverty has declined. Columbia University's Xavier Sala-i-Martin estimates that between 1976 and 1998, the number of people living on one dollar or less per day fell by 235 million. Further, the number living on two dollars or less per day fell by 450 million.[15] That is improvement worthy of our rejoicing!

How does it happen? Why has it happened so quickly in China and India, while much of Africa has grown slightly poorer over the same period, even as we have given massive amounts of foreign aid to Africa? Simply put, in places where markets operate freely, prices act as a signal—to all of us—to stop doing things that pay little and begin doing things that pay more. In the case of the coffee market, the reason that coffee continues to be cheap is that we keep making too much because we choose to ignore the price signal.

Putting at least some faith in markets to be a powerful force for change in the lives of the poor does not amount abdicating our concern for the poor, instead opting to cavalierly put our hope in little more than faeries and magic dust. Just as we trust gravity to keeps us all affixed securely to the ground, and just as principles of particle physics assure you that the chair you are sitting in right now will not let you slip through its seat to the floor, markets work invisibly in ways that we understand reasonably well. Although this author is no physicist, he trusts what a physicist tells him regarding what can and cannot work in our physical world, though the forces themselves cannot be easily observed; we see only the effects of such forces.

The laws of physics are part of God's providence; so are the laws of economics. In fact, many Christian economists have seen the providence of God in Adam Smith's famous invisible hand of the marketplace. Two quotes wonderfully and beautifully illustrate. Consider first the words of Robin Klay and John Lunn, two economics professors from Hope College in Holland, Michigan:

> Just as God-given productivity of the soil, combined with human labor and ingenuity, blesses societies with abundant crops, so also does the productivity of gifted human beings bless all humanity through markets. The somewhat mysterious way in which markets accomplish this without any one person directing it suggests to us the providential hand of God at work.[16]

More recently, in a book reflecting on John Calvin's thought regarding markets, David Hall and Matthew Burton write:

> God's providence is present in all events. We need to learn to see his "invisible hand" working in all things. He is truly sovereign over all of history. To doubt that is to reject God's lordship. Such repudiation is not merely based on an absence of information; it is also a rebellion of the heart against one's Creator. Happy is the person who learns to see God's hand in all of life.[17]

A key role for concerned Christians, then, is to permit and even encourage the power of markets to do the heavy lifting of the poor from poverty. One encouraging tool that is already making a difference in the lives of poor coffee and soybean growers is the Internet and mobile phone access. For years, coffee sellers everywhere and soybean growers in India have fallen victim to greedy middlemen by settling for a selling price that is below the going rate simply because growers did not have access to potential buyers other than their local coyote and also because they lacked accurate information regarding the going market value of their crops.

In a new piece of research, Aparajita Goyal presents significant evidence that the introduction of internet kiosks in the Indian state of Madhya Pradesh has allowed soybean farmers to access alternative marketing channels that had never before been available to them, as well as learn about current movements of soy prices. The presence of the kiosks has resulted in significantly higher soy prices, even after controlling for other potential explanatory factors.[18] In this case, it appears that the presence of kiosks has accomplished far more for poor soy farmers than any fair trade program could because the kiosks supplied valuable information that allowed the pricing system to work as intended. Sellers possessed reliable information about prices and traded accordingly. Philip Booth, writing for the *Catholic Times*, forecasts a similar role for mobile phones: "there are many other mechanisms [besides Fair Trade] around in the market for achieving similar objectives. Just to give one example, the mobile phone probably does more in Africa today to spread information about the best prices that primary producers can achieve than the fair trade movement. Its impact is tremendous."[19]

Speaking more generally, when poor countries grow rich, it rarely has anything at all to do with how many mouths they have to feed or the abundance of natural resources. Instead, across the globe, poor countries of all sizes, climates, and endowments begin to grow rich as two key factors increase. First, countries grow rich as their human capital improves. *Human capital* is the term economists use to describe the value that a country's people possess through their accumulated experience and education. For example, there is little doubt that India's recent growth explosion is due in large part to the education—including the knowledge of the English language—of its people. Second, countries grow rich as they invest in and accumulate *physical capital*: the machines, tools, infrastructure, and other equipment that make the product of each hour of physical labor more valuable.

That which both human capital and physical capital share is that they both transform the result of an hour of a person's hard work into something of even greater value. As the value of an hour of labor rises, employers gladly pay higher hourly rates, knowing that their bottom lines will be the better for it.

If we want to be effective agents in aiding the poor, we should focus our efforts in directions leading to the enhanced value of an hour of labor. That is, we should help poor countries wisely grow their stocks of human and physical capital, all the while bearing in mind that markets and their prices send the best available signals regarding where our efforts can have the greatest impact. The newfound success of innovative micro-lending efforts such as Kiva can help show us ways to effectively invest in the accumulation of physical capital by the global poor. Compassion International is a marvelous organization that works to further the education—the human capital—of poor children worldwide, with a financial accountability record above reproach.

Further, markets work best when economic systems maintain the dignity of human beings. Human beings grow and flourish—and accumulate human and physical capital—in systems that afford them considerable economic freedom. Economic freedom means that people are able to make personal choices, that their property is protected, and that they may voluntarily buy and sell in markets. Yet, economic freedom requires the protection of private property. When property rights are clearly defined and protected, people will work harder to create and to save. When they are confident that the fruits of their labors cannot be taken away arbitrarily or by force, people everywhere have greater assurance that their labors will lead to better lives for themselves and their families. Today's rich collection of NGOs that work toward basic human rights plays a critical role in this regard.

Finally, we should be outraged at the protectionist agricultural policies of already-rich nations such as the United States. When we allow the agricultural lobby to garner sweetheart deals from the U.S. House and Senate, the poor in other nations simply cannot compete with American growers of many crops because the trade rules are so utterly slanted against those in other nations. For example, it is illegal for sugar buyers in the United States to purchase their sugar from sources outside the United States, even though the world price of sugar lies below the federally mandated price of sugar in the United States. This is wonderful, though, for U.S. sugar beet growers in the United States; it means they have a captive supply of buyers at a price that is being kept artificially high by federal decree. If the United States were to abandon such self-centered policies, sugar growers everywhere would have access to our markets, and the price of sugar would fall for all of us. Moreover, confectioners and soft-drink makers in the United States would be able to produce their goods at lower costs, thereby adding to their job security. In one well-publicized case in 2002, Beatrice closed its Life-Savers factory in Holland, Michigan, and relocated to Canada, though the Michigan factory had been in operation for over thirty-five years and employed six hundred or so American workers. By moving to the northern side of the U.S.-Canada border, Life-Savers slashed its input costs dramatically because, in Canada, Life-Savers was free to buy cane sugar at the world price: sugar grown by those who need the income most.

Sugar is not the only market we currently protect to keep out lower-priced commodities in an effort to help poor farmers in the United States. We have erected similar barriers that turn a blind eye to the plight of the global poor in markets for cotton, peanuts, and several other products that we can grow at home. In fact, by now you can probably see another reason why coffee prices are low. Because coffee cannot be grown in Ohio, or in France, rich northerners have not erected protectionist barriers to keep out the coffee that foreigners make.

If we really care about the global poor, we should work to make trade freer for everyone in our global community: a level playing field for all. That means tearing down all of the barriers we use to keep the global poor from working in the very jobs in which they are perfectly positioned to make the greatest lasting gains.

Notes

1 All scripture quotations taken from the *New International Version*.
2 Jeremy Weber, "Fair Trade Coffee Enthusiasts Should Confront Reality," *Cato Journal* 27 (2007): 109.
3 Kate Bird and David R. Hughes, "Ethical Consumerism: The Case of 'Fairly-Traded' Coffee," *Business Ethics: A European Review* 6 (1997): 166.
4 Malgorzota Kurjanska and Mathias Risse, "Fairness in Trade II: Export Subsidies and the Fair Trade Movement," *Politics, Philosophy, & Economics* 7 (2008): 49.
5 *Economist*, "Voting with Your Trolley."
6 Ibid.
7 Margaret Levi and April Linton, "Fair Trade: A Cup at a Time?" *Politics & Society* 31 (2003): 420.
8 Brink Lindsey, "Grounds for Complaint? Understanding the 'Coffee Crisis,'" Trade Briefing Paper No. 16 (Washington, D.C.: Cato Institute, 2003), 6.
9 *Economist*, "Voting with Your Trolley."
10 John Wilkinson, "Fair Trade: Dynamic and Dilemmas of a Market Oriented Global Social Movement," *Journal of Consumer Policy* 20 (2007): 233.
11 Kurjanska and Risse, "Fairness in Trade II," 47.
12 Ibid., 46.
13 Collier, *Bottom Billion: Why the Poorest Countries Are Failing and What Can Be Done About It* (Oxford, U.K.: Oxford University Press, 2007), 163.
14 Tim Harford, *The Undercover Economist* (Oxford, U.K.: Oxford University Press, 2006), 229.

15 Robin Bade and Michael Parkin, *Foundations of Microeconomics*, 4th ed. (Boston: Addison-Wesley, 2009), 55.

16 Robin Klay and John Lunn, "The Relationship of God's Providence to Market Economies and Economic Theory," *Journal of Markets & Morality* 6 (2003): 559.

17 David W. Hall and Matthew D. Burton, *Calvin and Commerce: The Transforming Power of Calvinism in Market Economies* (Phillipsburg: P&R, 2009), 158.

18 Aparajita Goyal, "Information, Direct Access to Farmers, and Rural Market Performance in Central India," *American Economic Journal: Applied Economics* (forthcoming).

19 Philip Booth, "Fair Trade Proponents Should Have More Humility," *Catholic Times* (January 28, 2008), http://www.iea.org.uk/record.jsp?type=pressArticle&ID=350.

VI   Conclusion

We show our love for our Savior when we serve the poor. In Luke 10:27, our Lord gives us our marching orders for how we must show that love: "Love the Lord your God with all your heart and with all your soul and with all your strength and with all your mind."

Good intentions are marvelous, especially where the plight of the poor is concerned. The verse above does not stop after saying, "Love the Lord your God with all your heart and with all your soul." If it did, then fair trade might rise to the level of "good enough." We care much, we are doing something, and something is better than nothing.

The rest of the verse commands that we love our Lord—and by extension the poor—with all of our strength and with all of our minds. Notice the translation's use of the word *and*. Jesus does not command that we love him with some arbitrary combination of any or all of our hearts, *or* our souls, *or* our strength, *or* our minds. He commands that we serve him with all that we have, together with our minds.

By bringing the clear economic thinking of our minds to bear on the matters that tug hardest at our hearts and souls, we will serve him—and his children everywhere—as he commands. Caring for the global poor requires nothing less.

References and Further Reading

Arnot, Chris, Peter C. Boxall, and Sean B. Cash. 2006. "Do Ethical Consumers Care About Price? A Revealed Preference Analysis of Fair Trade Coffee Purchases." *Canadian Journal of Agricultural Economics* 54:555–65.

Bade, Robin, and Michael Parkin. 2009. *Foundations of Microeconomics*. 4th ed. Boston: Addison-Wesley.

Ballor, Jordan. 2009. "Critiquing Fair Trade and Dead Aid." Acton Institute PowerBlog. November 6. http://blog.acton.org/archives/12689-critiqu-ing-fair-trade-and-dead-aid.html.

———. 2004. "Strange Brew: Churches Push for 'Fair Trade' Coffee." Acton Commentary, February 3. http://www.acton.org/commentary/commentary_178.php.

Bates, Robert H. 1997. *Open-Economy Politics: The Political Economy of the World Coffee Trade*. Princeton: Princeton University Press.

Becchetti, Leonardo, and Furio Camillo Rosati. 2007. "Global Social Preferences and the Demand for Socially Responsible Products: Empirical Evidence from a Pilot Study on Fair Trade Consumers." *The World Economy* 30:807–36.

Bird, Kate, and David R. Hughes. 1997. "Ethical Consumerism: The Case of 'Fairly-Traded' Coffee." *Business Ethics: A European Review* 6:159–67.

Booth, Philip. 2009. "Don't Bully the Faithful into Buying Fairtrade." *Catholic Herald*. February 20. http://www.catholicherald.co.uk/features/opinion/o0000292.shtml.

———. 2008. "The Economics of Fair Trade: A Christian Perspective." 28th IEA Current Controversies Paper. Institute of Economic Affairs. London, UK.

———. 2008. "Fair Trade Proponents Should Have More Humility." *Catholic Times*. January 28. http://www.iea.org.uk/record.jsp?type=pressArticle&ID=350.

———. 2004. "Fairly Dangerous: The Church Takes a Stand against Free Traders." Acton Commentary. December 1. http://www.acton.org/commentary/commentary_231.php.

———. 2004. "Is Trade Justice Just? Is Fair Trade Fair?" IEA Discussion Paper No. 10, Institute of Economic Affairs, London, UK.

———. 2008. "Modern Business and Its Moral and Ethical Dilemmas in a Globalized World." In *Christian Theology and Market Economics*. Edited by Ian R. Harper and Samuel Gregg. Cheltenham, UK: Edward Elgar, 129–45.

Booth, Philip, and Linda Whetstone. 2007. "Half a Cheer for Fair Trade." *Economic Affairs* 27, no. 2: 29–36.

Collier, Paul. 2007. *The Bottom Billion: Why the Poorest Countries Are Failing and What Can Be Done About It*. Oxford: Oxford University Press.

Coren, Michael. 2005. "Christians Must Fight for Fair Trade." *Presbyterian Record*, May.

Economist. "Voting with Your Trolley." December 7, 2006.

Fridell, Gavin. 2007. *Fair Trade Coffee: The Prospects and Pitfalls of Market-Driven Social Justice*. Toronto: University of Toronto Press.

Gibbs, Eddie, and Ryan K. Bolger. 2005. *Emerging Churches: Creating Christian Community in Postmodern Cultures*. Grand Rapids: Baker Academic.

Goyal, Aparajita. "Information, Direct Access to Farmers, and Rural Market Performance in Central India." *American Economic Journal: Applied Economics* (forthcoming).

Hall, David W., and Matthew D. Burton. 2009. *Calvin and Commerce: The Transforming Power of Calvinism in Market Economies.* Phillipsburg: P&R.

Harford, Tim. 2006. *The Undercover Economist.* Oxford: Oxford University Press.

Harris, David. 2004. "Raise a Mug for Fair Trade." For the Record. *Presbyterian Record.* May 4.

Howley, Kerry. 2006. "Absolution in Your Cup: The Real Meaning of Fair Trade Coffee." *Reason.* March.

Joustra, Robert. 2009. "Fair Trade and Dead Aid: 'My Voice Can't Compete with an Electric Guitar.'" *Comment*, November 6. http://www.cardus.ca/comment/article/1234/.

Klay, Robin, and John Lunn. 2003. "The Relationship of God's Providence to Market Economies and Economic Theory." *Journal of Markets & Morality* 6:541–64.

Kurjanska, Malgorzata, and Mathias Risse. 2008. "Fairness in Trade II: Export Subsidies and the Fair Trade Movement." *Politics, Philosophy, & Economics* 7:29–56.

Larrivee, John. 2005. "Why Not Fair-Trade Beer and Cakes?" Acton Commentary. November 16. http://www.acton.org/commentary/commentary_296.php.

Levi, Margaret, and April Linton. 2003. "Fair Trade: A Cup at a Time?" *Politics & Society* 31:407–32.

Lindsey, Brink. 2003. "Grounds for Complaint? Understanding the 'Coffee Crisis.'" Trade Briefing Paper No. 16. Washington, D.C.: Cato Institute. http://www.cato.org/pub_display.php?pub_id=6807.

MacLachlan, Amy. 2005. "Mad About the Bean: Fair Trade Is Good to the Last Drop." *Presbyterian Record.* May, 20–24.

McLaren, Brian D. 2007. *Everything Must Change: Jesus, Global Crises, and a Revolution of Hope.* Nashville: Thomas Nelson.

Meadowcroft, John. 2005. "Fair Trade Will Lead to More Misery for Africa." *Yorkshire Post.* April 27. http://www.iea.org.uk/record.jsp?type=pressArticle&ID=179.

Miller, Michael. 2007. "Does Fair Trade Help the Poor?" Acton Commentary. October 31. http://www.acton.org/commentary/commentary411.php.

Munger, Mike. 2007. "Munger on Fair Trade and Free Trade: Interview with Russ Roberts." *EconTalk*. December 3. http://www.econtalk.org/archives/2007/12/munger_on_fair.html.

Pelsmacker, Patrick De, Liesbeth Driesen, and Glenn Rayp. 2005. "Do Consumers Care about Ethics? Willingness to Pay for Fair-Trade Coffee." *Journal of Consumer Affairs* 39:363–85.

Pendergrast, Mark. 1999. *Uncommon Grounds: The History of Coffee and How It Transformed Our World*. New York: Basic Books.

Richardson, Martin. 2007. "Fair Trade." Working Paper No. 31, Working Papers in Economics and Econometrics. Australian National University.

Singer, Peter, and Jim Mason. 2006. *The Way We Eat: Why Our Food Choices Matter*. Emmaus, Pa.: Rodale.

Smith, Adam. 1982. *The Theory of Moral Sentiments*. Edited by D. D. Raphael and A. L. Macfie. Vol. 1 of the Glasgow Edition of the Works and Correspondence of Adam Smith. Indianapolis: Liberty Fund.

Steinrücken, Torsten, and Sebastian Jaenichen. 2007. "The Fair Trade Idea: Towards an Economics of Social Labels." *Journal of Consumer Policy* 30:201–17.

———. 2006. "Does the Fair Trade Concept Work? An Economic Analysis of Social Labels." *Aussenwirtschaft* 61, no. 2: 189–210.

Wasserman, Miriam. 2002. "Trouble in Coffee Lands." *Regional Review* (Federal Reserve Bank of Boston) 12, no. 2: 4–13. http://www.bos.frb.org/economic/nerr/rr2002/q2/coffee.htm.

Watson, Matthew. 2007. "Trade Justice and Individual Consumption Choices: Adam Smith's Spectator Theory and the Moral Constitution of the Fair Trade Consumer." *European Journal of International Relations* 13:263–88.

Weber, Jeremy. 2007. "Fair Trade Coffee Enthusiasts Should Confront Reality." *Cato Journal* 27:109–17.

Weitzman, Hal. 2006. "Bitter Cost of 'Fair Trade' Coffee: An *FT* Investigation Finds Premium Price Beans Are Picked by Workers Paid Below Minimum Wage." *Financial Times*. September 9.

———. 2006. "'Ethical-Coffee' Workers Paid Below Legal Minimum." *Financial Times*. September 9.

Wilkinson, John. 2007. "Fair Trade: Dynamic and Dilemmas of a Market Oriented Global Social Movement." *Journal of Consumer Policy* 20:219–39.

About the Authors

VICTOR V. CLAAR is professor of economics at Henderson State University, Arkansas, where he specializes in teaching principles of economics courses. He holds a bachelor's degree in business administration from Houghton College in New York, where he completed a second major in mathematics. He earned his master's and Ph.D. in economics at West Virginia University, where he wrote his doctoral dissertation under the guidance of Ronald Balvers. Prior to arriving at Henderson, he held the tenured rank of associate professor of economics at Hope College, Michigan, where he taught from 2000–2009. Professor Claar spent the 2006–2007 academic year as a Fulbright Scholar in Armenia—a poor former Soviet republic—giving graduate lectures and conducting research at the American University of Armenia. His book with Robin J. Klay, *Economics in Christian Perspective: Theory, Policy, and Life Choices*, was published in 2007 by IVP Academic, the scholarly imprint of InterVarsity Press. His scholarly articles have appeared in several peer-reviewed outlets, including *Applied Economics*, *Public Finance Review*, and the *Journal of Markets & Morality*. He also serves regularly on the faculty of Acton University. Professor Claar is the son of a retired pastor in the United Methodist Church, though his membership is currently in the Episcopal Church. Before moving to Arkansas, his church home was Trinity Lutheran Church in Grand Rapids, Michigan.

MICHAEL W. KRUSE lives with his wife, Melissa, in Midtown Kansas City, Missouri. He is the author of the Kruse Kroncile blog where he explores ongoing developments relating to the Church, economics, and discipleship. He is an elder in the Presbyterian Church U.S.A. and will be serving as chair of the General Assembly Mission Council from 2010–2012. He has had a longstanding interest in micro-economic development. Since 1994, he has volunteered with First Step Fund, a program of the Kauffman Foundation, helping disadvantaged persons develop feasibility studies and secure funding for small businesses. He recently joined the board of a new Christian organization called Significant Matters, which has as one of its goals linking people with business acumen to micro-enterprise efforts in emerging nations.

povertycure
From aid to enterprise

Statement of Principles

The Challenge of Global Poverty

We are called to a loving and generous concern for the poor. Yet for many of us with a heart for the poor, the statistics are almost overwhelming. More than a billion people live on less than $1.25 a day. Every year, millions of men, women, and children die from AIDS, malaria, and other preventable diseases. Tens of millions lack clean water and go to bed hungry.

There is, however, reason for hope. Although we cannot create heaven on earth, we know what it takes for the poor to be able to create new wealth for themselves and rise out of poverty. Indeed, there exist powerful tools that could allow us to make enormous strides in creating prosperous societies. It is time to rethink poverty. It is time to put the person, made in the image of God, at the center of the economy. It is time to help unleash the entrepreneurial spirit of the developing world.

The PovertyCure Vision

When we put the person at the center of our economic thinking, we transform the way we look at wealth and poverty. Instead of asking what causes poverty, we begin to ask, what causes wealth? What are the conditions for human flourishing from which prosperity can grow? And how can we create and protect the space for people to live out their freedom and responsibilities?

It is time to move:

- From aid to enterprise
- From poverty alleviation to wealth creation
- From paternalism to partnerships
- From handouts to investments
- From seeing the poor as consumers or burdens to seeing them as creators
- From viewing people and economies as experiments to pursuing solidarity with the poor
- From viewing the poor as recipients of charity to acknowledging them as agents of change with dignity, capacity, and creativity
- From encouraging dependency to integrating the poor into networks of productivity and exchange
- From subsidies and protectionism to open trade and competition
- From seeing the global economy as a fixed pie to understanding that human enterprise can grow economies

Charity, Global Poverty, and Christian Tradition

The Judeo-Christian tradition has always emphasized solidarity with the poor. But solidarity means more than simply providing relief. It means viewing the poor as partners and joining together with them in networks of productivity and exchange. Charity and almsgiving play an indispensable role in our efforts to help the poor, and yet the goal for charitable organizations should be to help the poor move beyond dependency. No country ever became wealthy and self-sufficient through foreign assistance—public or private. In the long run, sustainable supplies of food, clean water, health, and education are created by local wealth-creating economies integrated into interdependent networks.

Christians have always been involved in helping the poor through charity, almsgiving, and service. In recent decades, Christians have sometimes looked to large, secular political entities and international organizations as the key for helping the poor. This is an understandable but inadequate response. First, many of these groups begin with a mistaken vision of the human person. If we are going to help the poor, we must first understand the nature, calling, and destiny of human beings. Second, despite many good intentions, large-scale foreign-aid plans have been largely ineffective. Trillions of dollars in aid over the last sixty years have been unable to lift the poorest countries out of extreme poverty. It is time to change.

A Cultural Treasury

There is no single Christian way of fighting poverty. Christians are called to serve in numerous ways, and good people will disagree about a host of prudential questions when addressing poverty. However, if we are to do more good than harm, we must begin with a biblical vision of the human person. This is the challenge for all of us, wherever we fall on the political and economic spectrum.

This is not a call to embrace a spirituality detached from physical reality. Just the opposite; the God of the universe is concerned about culture, is concerned about history, is concerned about physicality because he is concerned about the humanity that he made. Good intentions are not enough. In the words of philosopher Etienne Gilson, "Piety is never a substitute for technique."

To be clear, Christianity is principally concerned with saving souls and making disciples of all nations. This in no way negates the fact that God also calls us to help the poor escape the ravages of material poverty. Moreover, we know that our earthly vocations have a double task: to fill the earth and rule over it, and this universal calling of God urges us to create space for rich and poor alike to live out their freedom and responsibility as stewards of creation.

It is also important to emphasize that a Christian approach to development does not preclude our working with people from other faiths and traditions. Many nonbelievers of good will share core beliefs with us about human dignity and the root causes of poverty. We need Christians working within and beside secular organizations focused on alleviating extreme poverty. This is honorable work, and the call to approach poverty alleviation from a fully Christian perspective does place certain demands on Christians working in development. Many development organizations are shaped by mistaken visions of the person. Sadly, even some Christian groups end up advocating programs that clash with foundational aspects of the Christian theological and moral tradition, such as the call to protect human life at all stages. As followers of Christ, we must guard against unwittingly adopting the current secular framework.

Christians have been the largest and most powerful force for helping the poor the world has ever known, and many of the institutions of both charity and wealth creation sprang up from the soil of the Christian tradition. It is important to cultivate a robust appreciation of this tradition and to emphasize the effective tools in our cultural treasury for helping the poor to flourish. These include:

- *Development is about more than GDP.* It is about integral human flourishing. With its rich vision of the good life and by emphasizing the everlasting destiny of the person, Christianity steers us away from both hopelessness and arid utilitarianism.

- *Every human person possesses inherent dignity and worth.* The Judeo-Christian tradition teaches that all humans are made in the image of the Creator. We are, therefore, beings with a transcendent destiny, beings of purpose, reason and creativity, able to make free choices. Although many Christians throughout the centuries have ignored this fundamental teaching, it continues to call people to recognize the inherent dignity and worth of every human person, including those outside our own clan, tribe, or nation.

- *We cannot create heaven on earth.* Guided by sound ideas and principles, as well as a rich moral culture, we can greatly reduce global poverty. Scripture, the Christian tradition, and the reality of human sin warn us against any worldly plan that promises to fashion "a new man" and achieve a perfect society. Within human history the ideal situation will never exist. There will always be poverty because there will always be tragedy and sin. This does not justify complacency toward our fellow man, but it should warn us against any plan that promises to "end poverty" or any political ideology that promises perfect equality or justice. As history has shown us, every political promise of the perfect society leads not to liberation but enslavement.

- *Although made in the image of God, humanity is fallen.* Many approaches to fighting poverty take too little account of human sinfulness, leading to a lack of accountability and, with it, corruption, waste, and more poverty. We must avoid a utopianism that ignores the reality of sin.

- *Honest labor, including the work of business, is a dignified and moral activity.* As creatures made in the image of God, creative labor helps us develop our full humanity. This extends to enterprise and business. While the Bible warns of the dangers, the parable of the talents and other biblical passages have encouraged the Church since ancient times to view honest business, including making a profit, as an opportunity for human flourishing.

- *We should practice effective compassion.* Business enterprise is the normal way that poor communities move from poverty to prosperity. Yet the need for almsgiving to assist the poor will always be a component of development, even essential in certain circumstances. Here effective compassion is vital. We must avoid being satisfied with making visible, feel-good charitable gestures, not least because the Christian tradition insists this is not enough. Christianity calls us not only to give to those in need, but to do so in an intelligent way, so that our giving does not do unintended harm. A heart for the poor is important, but one also needs a mind for the poor.

- *No human ruler is above the law.* Christianity teaches that the ruler is subject to the divine moral order; neither power nor consensus equals truth. This is crucial for political and economic freedom and human flourishing.

- **_Government has an important, limited role._** Christianity emphasizes the core competency of government—securing justice for rich and poor alike, which creates space for human flourishing. This translates into upholding rule of law and private property rights and allowing for free association, and free and honest exchange. While government is important, Christianity emphasizes that it is not the only entity that gives society its identity. Individuals, families, churches, private organizations, businesses, charities, and government all play essential roles in building a healthy society and must act according to the principle of subsidiarity.

- **_We are stewards of creation with freedom and responsibility._** The earth is a gift to be developed responsibly. The stewardship approach to creation encourages holistic and sustainable development. On the one hand, it cautions us against crass and hedonistic exploitation of the natural realm. On the other hand, it warns us away from viewing nature as divine, or the earth as a sanctuary to be left undeveloped.

- **_The family is a core building block of society._** Empirical data from numerous sources show that strong families are crucial to sustainable economic development. We must be careful not to promote approaches to development that lead to family breakdown. Christians, along with people from other religious traditions that emphasize strong families, should counter the excessive individualism of Western secular culture, an individualism that sees the family as inessential or marginal to integral human development. Christianity helps to steer us away from this costly error by showing that the family is a prepolitical institution, ordained by God from the beginning.

- **_Vibrant communities and private associations are essential to liberty and the common good._** The Christian tradition emphasizes the principle of subsidiarity. This is the idea that social and economic problems should be solved by those closest to them whenever possible (i.e., the family, the church and neighborhood, the community), making temporary recourse to more distant levels of assistance only when necessary and with deep awareness of the dangers of institutionalizing detached and distant forms of bureaucratic assistance. Strong communities and voluntary associations—not linked to the state—play a key role in making economic development humane and sustainable.

- *The rights and responsibilities of private property must be supported.* One of the crucial lessons of development economics is that the poor cannot create wealth for themselves and their families without secure property rights. The Judeo-Christian tradition provides powerful resources for encouraging the property rights of rich and poor alike. It shows that private property is not an artifact of greed and possessiveness, as many believe, but rather a legitimate institution rooted in our role as stewards of what God has entrusted to each of us.

- *Culture matters.* Christianity reminds us that poverty alleviation is not primarily a resource problem. Wealth creation requires a cultural context. Corrupt regimes in developing countries stifle initiative while developed countries all too often manipulate and cripple poor countries, sometimes by means of the very aid programs we had hoped would break the cycle of poverty. Societies that enable human flourishing require cultures that promote trust, honesty, reasoned discourse, and respect for the dignity of the person.

PovertyCure Goals

- Promote the dignity of the person and the family.
- Shift the locus of responsibility from international organizations to the poor themselves.
- Encourage vibrant communities and voluntary civil associations—distinct from the state—because they are crucial for authentic human flourishing and help build solidarity.

- Build and encourage institutions of private property, rule of law, free association, free exchange, and a culture of trust, which serve to (1) free the poor to connect to networks of productivity and exchange, (2) create a positive climate for business and entrepreneurship, (3) promote the freedom to pursue productive work free of oppression and theft, and (4) promote a culture of enterprise that unleashes human potential.

- Promote authentic respect for the health and dignity of women and children from conception to natural death.

- Promote free, honest, and competitive market economies— not oligarchic or crony capitalism.

- Create conditions and institutions that allow people in regions of extreme poverty to develop ready access to clean water and sustain it.

- End the subsidies, cartels, and protectionist policies of the developed world. They hurt the poor, protect the wealthy from competition, give unfair advantage to big business, and facilitate corruption.

- Shift the focus in the development community away from government-to-government transfers and toward face-to-face partnerships informed by local knowledge and marked by mutual respect and understanding.

- Free up developing countries to combat malaria and other diseases using the same effective tools the developed world has used to eradicate diseases.

- Reject neocolonial presumptions that the poor are helpless and cultivate respectful, mutually beneficial working relationships between Christians from the developed and developing worlds.

PovertyCure Insights

There is no magic bullet for the poverty that plagues many nations, but history teaches us some of the important factors necessary to create wealth.

- The economy is not a fixed pie or zero-sum game where people can only get richer if they take from someone else. History and economics teaches that economies can grow and one person's wealth does not mean another's impoverishment.

- Malthusian predictions of overpopulation have proven false again and again. Population does not cause poverty. "Besides the earth, man's principal resource is man himself." (*Centesimus Annus*)

- Poor countries grow economically when they are allowed to compete in the global economy and are linked to networks of productivity and circles of exchange.

- Honest competition within a moral framework creates opportunity for the poor.

- Business and entrepreneurship are keys to prosperity and economic growth.

- Transparent and competitive markets, within a moral framework are beneficial to the poor. A market economy requires, among other things, certain formal and informal institutions in order to be just and sustainable. These include private property rights and the rule of law for rich and poor alike, the consistent enforcement of contracts, free association and free exchange for everyone and not just for the privileged few, a culture of trust, vibrant community life, and a rich vision of man that goes beyond homo-economicus or man as rational maximizer. We recognize that no market economy will ever be perfectly just, but where these institutions are weak or missing, the poor are especially harmed. In order to effectively encourage human flourishing, efforts must be made to foster these institutions.

- Good economic development is sustainable and should be environmentally sensitive.
- Economic progress is the fastest path to an economically and environmentally sustainable future.
- People have a right to migrate in search of new opportunities. This dovetails into the Christian provision to love the immigrants among us.
- Liberty is more than the right to exercise one's will. True liberty is achieved by acting in accordance with truth and reason. Freedom for excellence is achieved through hard work and discipline.
- People have the natural right of free association. They should be allowed to form businesses, charities, schools, unions, and NGOs without facing suffocating regulation.
- The West needs to move away from a neocolonial vision that views people in the developing world as helpless children.
- Nations and cultures have the right to resist radical secularist morality.
- The free market is not government in cahoots with big business. This is the unhealthy subversion of free markets and free competition.
- Developing countries may have sound reasons to pursue short-term protection of an industry, but long-term import substitution policies are ineffective and reduce opportunity for the poor.

The Church's Role in Combating Global Poverty

- Preach the Gospel—the most transforming force in history.
- Preach a holistic vision of Christian stewardship.
- Speak out against exploitation and corruption.

- Provide moral guidance, encouraging the development of virtues needed to create the conditions for human flourishing and prosperity.
- Help create social bonds and fight anonymity.
- Build a rich moral ecology and a culture of trust.
- Assist its members into economic independence by encouraging job training, financial planning, and career development.
- Provide a deep sense of rootedness.
- Help members understand that many of the institutions essential to sustainable and equitable prosperity grew out of the Christian tradition.
- Offer charity in targeted and intelligent ways that encourage human flourishing rather than dependency and cultural decay.

Christian evangelism has the power to lift up the poor. By focusing on the priceless work of making disciples of all nations, Christian missionaries lay the groundwork for profound cultural transformation, for the ideas, attitudes, and institutions that allow for human flourishing, including wealth creation among the poor.

PovertyCure: Take Action

- Think before you act.
- Think biblically.
- Pray and seek wise counsel.
- Realize that good intentions alone do not solve poverty.
- Learn the fundamental truths of economics.
- Get involved: educate yourself on the principles of effective compassion and then put the principles into action, using your time, talents, and resources.
- Educate others about the principles of effective compassion.

- Investigate the charitable institutions you are considering supporting and hold them accountable for practicing effective compassion.
- If you have relevant expertise, consider looking for ways to invest in business in the developing world, perhaps through organizations that specialize in identifying promising small- and medium-sized enterprises or in extending microcredit—providing micro financial services. As with charitable giving, study before you invest, holding the organizations or investment recipients to high standards of moral probity and business competence.
- Join the PovertyCure Network and spread the word.